A Short Introduction to Risk Assessment

Also by Edmund J Fish

A Short Introduction to Risk Assessment – Part 1 – The Building
Blocks

In Preparation

Overpressure Protection – A 21st Century Approach to Relief
System Designing
The Management Assumption – Why the Workers are Revolting
The Personal Edge – A Companion Guide to the Management
Assumption
Building a Better Mousetrap – Understanding Project
Management
Designing a Better Mousetrap – Innovation and New Product
Development
The Money Factory – Process Improvement for Everyone

A Short Introduction to Risk Assessment

Part 2 – Why They are Always WRONG

by Edmund J Fish

Notes on the cover illustration by Chloe Green:

There are subtle clues in the cover illustration that are worthy of mention.

Death's horse is shying away, uncertain of its direction; and the question mark brand indicates uncertainty.

Famine's horse is wearing blinkers, to show it has restricted vision; and the heart shaped brand indicates thinking with emotions rather than logic.

Pestilence's horse has a complex bridle, which is obscured in the final version; and the cogs brand symbolises the complex modern world.

War's horse concept of "is it there or not" did not translate well into the final colour scheme; however, the Necker's cube brand indicates the ambiguity of data.

Dedication

This book is dedicated to my children George, Emily, David and Matthew. They have been teachers about much in life; not least what it means to perceive risk from a different perspective

This page is intentionally blank (or not)

Table of Contents

Table of Figures

Foreword

I met Ed in 2008 during discussions to improve CCPS's chemical reactivity hazard management tool. We have stayed connected due to our shared interest in the challenge in helping to get to grips with risk analysis. In this articulate book, aimed at risk professionals and other interested parties, Ed makes a significant contribution to the vision of a risk-literate society. This is essential as public understanding of risk is very low. Unless risk professionals engage others in understanding risk analysis, management, and decision making, work in the area of process safety may never achieve its full maturity and potential.

During the latter part of my tenure as Executive Director of the Center for Chemical Process Safety (CCPS), we undertook an exercise to envision the future of process safety. In this future, the obstacles that challenge us daily have been removed and the enablers of process safety were all in place. The result – Vision 20/20 – is described in detail on the CCPS website. Perhaps the most surprising obstacle uncovered during this exercise was the need for there to be a much better understanding of risk across society, not just by a few risk analysts sitting in industrial and academic ivory towers.

Certainly, understanding risk is critical for making informed decisions about manufacturing processes, considering their potential harm to people, profitability, and the environment. But it is equally important for companies to be able to have productive conversations with their industrial neighbors, regulators, and legislators. Today, when these conversations occur, it seems that none of the parties understands risk. So conversations start with the public saying "Eliminate all risk" and the company saying "trust us, we know what we are doing." Depending on the political winds, such conversations end either with a stalemate or an awkward and ineffective regulation.

Imagine instead a world where risk is not treated as an esoteric mathematical subject but instead taught from the time students have learned basic mathematical concepts. In this world, people would recognize the difference between a risk perception and an actual risk. They would recognize what helps reduce risk and what is only whitewash. In this world, business and society could have all manner of discussions about risk, and reach more sensible and practical agreements about how to control risks.

In this book, Ed strives to help readers understand risk and dispel misconceptions about it. In doing so, he is contributing to this future vision of a risk-literate society. For sure, this book is intended for professionals, not secondary school level students. However, it should help professionals speak about risk more clearly, and this addresses a key part of the challenge. I commend him for taking on this important task.

Scott Berger
Former Executive Director of the CCPS

Preface

In Volume 1 – The Building Blocks, we learnt that conducting or completing a risk assessment is a (comparatively) simple task. The generation of the scenario and the assigning of likelihoods is not an impossible task to understand. What inspired this book was the experience of people misunderstanding what risk assessments truly are. In addition, we have come to believe an over simplified model, and why our own mental biases sometimes lead us to miss the obvious and lay the seeds of our very own confusion.

This book will not help you fix these problems, but it will help you understand why risk assessments are for guiding decisions, not the answer to the question of what to do; although we will look at how people still make remarkably good decisions despite all this.

Introduction

In Volume 1 we looked at how to create a risk assessment and we defined risk as the *expected value* of likelihood (or frequency) times the level of harm. Surely after that we have set out the definition of risk?

The reality is that expressing risk is a much more nuanced concept and we need to review how we look at risk. The vagary of risk is made of many parts, yet the whole is simple to understand. The conundrum was whether to start with the parts or the whole.

In the end it was decided to introduce the overview of why it gets confusing. Then we will review how we conceptualise risk, both linguistically and mathematically in the context of the overview.

This is followed by a look at our mental process that can lead the assessment astray, both due to underlying psychological biases, as well as errors that we can make from normal human mistakes and how they contribute to the inaccuracy of risk assessment. We'll take a look at how we handle the *Four Horsemen of the Apocalypse*; or the four types of uncertainty in making decisions. We could add an extension to the subtitle of this book making it, *Why They Are Always Wrong and How We Cope*.

The reader that survives the onslaught will be rewarded by an example of a risk assessment about a pipeline that shows how the *Four Horsemen* ride into the most reasonable decision. Their presence will be so obvious that we discover that they have hidden in plain sight all these years.

At the end of the book the reader should have an understanding of the vagaries of talking about risk. The limits of risk assessment should be clear and how to use them sensibly to guide decision will be clarified. You'll discover there are limits on the ways to make

1

risk assessments better or more accurate; and an appreciation of limits of human decision making, even with the best possible risk assessments.

Risk is not a complex subject, but it does need careful study. Risk is made up of a several simple concepts that interact, but the one that causes us the greatest problems is uncertainty. It is this complex, emotional relationship we have with uncertainty that troubles our understanding of risk. What we want is clear, casino or laboratory probability with predictable outcomes.

The roots of misunderstanding risk and uncertainty are included in this book and we shall explore them in sufficient depth, so that those wanting a greater depth of understanding can delve into more detailed texts with confidence.

Chapter 1
Uncertainty:
Riding the Four Horsemen?

Many may take umbrage with the idea that we have declared that all risk assessments, and by inference the basis for all decisions, are wrong. It is not a statement made lightly. The reason that risk assessments are wrong is because they are not conducted in the sterile environment of the laboratory, but in the messy real world, which contains uncertainty.

ISO 73 – Risk Management – Vocabulary, defines risk as "the uncertainty on objectives". This is in contrast to our definition in Part 1 of likelihood of harm, which is in line with ISO 51. These two definitions are in conflict, and this book aims to explain why, in truth, both are wrong. Others have proposed more complex descriptions of risk, but are only trying to include the truth that risk is both positive and negative. With definitions being wrong, or at least lacking clarity, there is little doubt that risk assessment will be wrong.

Frank Knight described uncertainty to be separate from risk; in short, he stated that uncertainty is separate from the evaluation of risk. Whilst this might be true uncertainty is more integral to a risk assessment than that statement might imply. You cannot separate uncertainty from a risk assessment and we need to understand why.

To begin our journey we need to return to a much maligned speech by Donald Rumsfeld. In that speech he referred to the 'known knowns', 'known unknowns' and the 'unknown unknowns'. Despite the derision this speech often receives it is, in fact, an excellent summary of the nature of uncertainty and of the many ways it influences risk assessments and the decisions we make based on them.

The 'known knowns' are things we feel we know with certainty. How much we feel we know all there is to be known the more confident we are, and that can create problems, which we shall discuss later in the book. We are, also, deluding ourselves because there is uncertainty lurking even in the things we think we know. We shall reveal this uncertainty throughout this book.

The 'known unknowns' are those groups of things we feel we can quantify without detailing the data. This is common in preparing project cost estimates, a form of risk estimate that an activity/project will cost a certain amount. Uncertainty still lurks here, and we can be over-confident in this area by convincing ourselves that these are, in fact, 'known knowns' because we can quantify them.

Finally, we come to the 'unknown unknowns'. By their very nature we don't know these things. However, this is the place where we exclusively believe that uncertainty resides. Although our knowledge here is, by definition, uncertain it is not the only source of uncertainty. Before we take a closer look at uncertainty,

in all its guises, we need to look at our relationship with
uncertainty.

Why Feel So Unsure about Uncertainty

When we talk about uncertainty we are thinking of it as a "bad
thing", that it is singularly undesirable. Why are we convinced
that it is so bad? The truth is that comes down to how it makes us
feel.

When we talk about uncertainty it evokes emotions such as
bravery, inspiration, hope, challenge, determination, anxiety,
concern, distress, nervousness, frustration, apathy, pressure,
confusion, helplessness, outrage, cheated, distraught, panicked,
burdened, flustered, scared, sad, shocked, overwhelmed, or
ambivalent. The list is dominated by negative emotions, but if we
distil them all down they are either fight or flight; a play on our
rudimentary reaction to fear.

The reason uncertainty creates this fear is because it generates at
least two possible futures/outcomes, which tend to be mutually
exclusive. In psychology this is referred to as a *cognitive
dissonance*. The human mind does not like to hold mutually
exclusive concepts and we will create a story that resolves this to a
single consistent outcome. The way we do this is not the subject of
this book, but as we show below it is like energy because
uncertainty can only be transformed from one form to another.

This immediate link to 'fear' undoubtedly has some link to our
sense of *loss aversion* and our sense of *relative loss*. Both of these
reactions/behaviours are linked to our programmed sense of
survival, where it is more important not to be killed by a predator
than it is to not miss a meal [Fish 9(a)]. We all prefer the option
that ensures we survive. This is known as the *negativity bias*

where we are hardwired to detect danger. Grossly simplifying the matter, we have specific regions of the brain that sense danger and none that sense safety. Hence, we are able to assess/detect a dangerous situation five times faster than concluding another situation is safe.

Thus, if a loss is small, or inconsequential, we may appear to adopt unusual risk seeking behaviour because it is not 'life threatening'. The experience of 'throwing good money after bad' and gambling addiction are other psychological functions that we will ignore when considering a normal decision [Fish (a)].

Although there is potential to discuss our visceral response to risk, the connection is fundamentally with fear. No matter how hard we push for an objective response to risk, our reaction to uncertainty will always be one of fear. This awareness alone may allow us to make more logical decisions.

We can be confident that we 'know the knowns' and have defined the risk. Our confidence may, or may not, be misplaced. What is certain is that we need a way to assess uncertainty and balance our confidence when making decisions. For that we need to have a better understanding of the reasons of why we are unsure about uncertainty.

Why Are We So Unsure about Uncertainty

If there are so many sources of uncertainty, why do we find it so hard to recognise? There are a number of reasons and they range from the nature of the universe to human psychology. These are, also, not always easy to separate. How do we find the 'unknown unknowns'?

One school of thought is based in physics. The Heisenberg Uncertainty Principle states that there is a limit to how accurately we can know something. There is undoubted truth in this, but it applies to such a small scale that it is unlikely to be a major influence on probabilities. The exception might be if we are examining micro-scale events where a single or few molecules could change events. In most cases the macro behaviour of a piece of pipe or a pool of liquid will not be that greatly influenced by these microscopic events.

In *Black Swan* Naseem Taleb argues strongly against invoking Heisenberg. His argument is both right and wrong. He is dismissive of the relevance of this type of uncertainty and as noted in Chapter 2 in terms of practical application, it is a red herring. However, the underlying concept is still valid if we consider that we can either know the outcome or we can know the likelihood; in Chapter 2 we will talk about adding a 'blob' to the risk matrix. As we tend to focus on the likelihood of the event we see one dimensional variation rather than two dimensions.

Dr. Taleb's point is another point we expand in Chapter 2. We often assume the wrong type of distribution for the likelihood; if we assume one at all. We tend to assume a Gaussian distribution, but *power law distributions* are more common than we think and these curves have 'long tails' (see Figure 1). Figure 1 shows only one side of the distributions and demonstrates how the likelihood of an event (y-axis) is for unusual type events (further left on the x-axis). Note that the 'expectedly more common events' are less likely than we imagine. Thus, there are more 'rare' events due to the 'long tails' of *power law distributions* than we expect. Again, we note in Chapter 2 that work by John Hollman suggests a log-normal curve is more often the case and there may be events that cause the distribution to change shape and mean.

We ignore these 'unknown unknowns' as a matter of course. We don't know them, so we operate without any means of explicitly, or logically, expressing them. Dealing with this is something we shall return to later. Now the question is when can we be so sure about uncertainty?

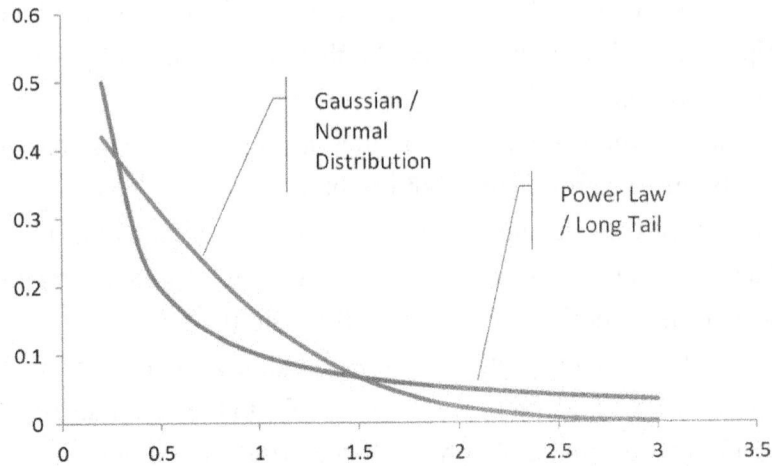

Figure 1 - Power Law and Gaussian Distributions

When We Are So Sure about Uncertainty

As we have mentioned, there is a strong tendency to believe in the validity of *faux science*; or the fact that because someone has produced a very accurate number, we believe that this number is accurate. There is a reason we feel this way, and it relates to how we feel about the implicit uncertainty.

These hard numbers give us a sense of having quantified the 'known knowns' and boxed off the 'known unknowns'. Our confidence is derived from having defined and quantified the 'known knowns'. It creates a certainty in what we know and we tend to filter out or minimise our sense of uncertainty.

8

Our confidence in knowing the knowns can trigger biases and exaggerate our misconceptions of risk. Confidence can lead us to be strident about our decision. Even the 'known knowns' may be subjective; consider for example expert, subjective judgement of values.

The boundary between 'known unknowns' and 'unknown unknowns' can start to become blurred. Hard numbers may make the 'known unknowns' seem as if they are under control, but it is the 'unknown-ness' of them that may come to be the downfall of the decision.

The root of this confidence is in how uncertainty makes us feel. The application of hard; emotionless numbers ameliorates that feeling, but it cannot be ignored. In short, we are afraid when we are unsure of something.

Even when we are sure we know everything, or even that we know what we don't know, there is uncertainty in what we do know. That uncertainty is lurking everywhere in our risk assessments. It comes in four shades, the Four Horsemen of the Apocalypse, which herald our downfall from a bad decision due to uncertainty.

Meet the Four Horsemen

Various forms of uncertainty have been alluded to by John Hollman in his works for the *Association for the Advancement of Cost Engineering* (AACE International). Uncertainty comes in four general forms, which I have associated with the Four Horsemen of the Apocalypse. We all work better with strong imagery and the idea that uncertainty can lead to an apocalyptic decision creates a strong anchor for our memory. As it transpires there is a tenuous link with the nature of each horseman and the forms of uncertainty. So, without further ado let's meet uncertainty.

In the Book of Revelations there are Four Horsemen associated with the coming of the Apocalypse; Death, Famine, Pestilence, and War. Each is associated with a form of uncertainty as follows:

1. Death   = uncertainty (covers all uncertainty)
2. Famine   = subjectivity
3. Pestilence = complexity
4. War   = ambiguity

The list above is ordered in the sequence that the horsemen are generally recognised. However, we are likely to recognise the forms of uncertainty in the reverse order and that is the order we will examine them in below.

War

War is about conflict and ambiguity is a conflict of two (at least) ideas that are usually mutually exclusive. Psychologically this is often referred to as *cognitive dissonance*. Later in the book we will look at the steps the human mind takes to remove this ambiguity that can lead to poor risk assessments and/or poor decisions.

An example of ambiguity would be when two sets of numerical data exist for failure frequencies for items. Which data set is the 'correct' one? If one group uses one set and the other group the other set they will get different values of risk. Who is right? It's unclear, but we'll make our own decision to remove the ambiguity.

Another form of ambiguity can be when we compare forms of harm. Is that loss of earnings or damage to equipment really equal to the loss of a human life? This example itself is proof of the confusion about uncertainty. Remember it and ask yourself how it fits with the next two horsemen.

The danger of War's ambiguity is that we use self-serving biases that resolve that ambiguity in our favour; whichever way that may be. Thus, those in favour of taking an action and believe a risk is worth taking will find reasons to do so, whereas those against will find reasons not to.

Pestilence

Pestilence can be defined as an infectious disease that infects a whole community. Complexity, according to Cynefin, is a system where the relationships are only clear with experience, or hindsight. These complex interrelationships infect the analysis by hiding chains of events that only seem obvious after an incident. Alternatively, complexity in a risk assessment leads to repeating work to clarify the relationships; usually resulting in the revelation of more complexity. The same can be seen in projects, with what is referred to as *emergent behaviour*.

Complexity typically arises from *disjunctive* events; where either A or B, as well as A and B are all possible outcomes (see the type of harm example for ambiguity). The complexity tends to rise exponentially, just consider the effect of one more potential, non-exclusive outcome C.

The combinations rise in number the more events there are and how do we simplify this complexity without losing its impact? Any efforts to simplify blur the risk and compound this by introducing ambiguity; merely trading one form of uncertainty for another, so spreading the infection of uncertainty.

Pestilence's complexity is likely to cause mental confusion; we typically resolve this by considering the complex outcomes to be ambiguous. This leads us back to the self-serving biases again

11

where we simplify the issues ignoring those that do not favour the action we support.

Famine

Famine is the scarcity of 'food'. The food for any risk assessment is objective data. However, there is no objective data for every type of event. What do we do when there is no objective data?

Without objective data the assessor will make a subjective assessment and create a quantification based on experience, or analogy. Different people may have different *subjective* values that they feel are suitable. There are no right or wrong, or even ambiguous, answers and we are uncertain what we truly know.

The presence of numbers can disguise these assumptions and we become subject to the illusion *faux science*, where we ignore the uncertainty because a number is present and we place faith in the number without considering its source. The more subjective data used in a risk assessment the more complex the unknowns become and more ambiguity creeps into the data.

As before, ambiguity has entered our processing of the information and we will return to the self-serving biases to support our decision. Despite our efforts we have returned to conflict over the information, and data, involved in the risk assessment.

Death

Every other form of uncertainty is covered by Death, including those noted above. When uncertainty is readily identifiable in the risk assessment then its value as a decision aid is dead. No party will place any value on a piece of information that does not inspire a minimum level of confidence. War, Pestilence and Famine are not the only forms of uncertainty and Death brings its own set of uncertainties to scythe down the confidence of the risk assessment.

A brief list of some of the other forms of uncertainty is given below. Why they cause uncertainty, as well as other forms of uncertainty, are discussed later in the book.

1. Treating all risks as (potential) losses,
2. Ignoring the subjective value placed on the value of the outcomes, the risk value is a moral/ethical question,
3. Ignoring that likelihood is a distribution, not a point value,
4. Ignoring the shape of the likelihood distribution,
5. Assuming that the values used are from a large population,
6. Treating all elements of the scenario as having an equal impact on the variability of the risk,
7. Not appreciating that the answer is only as good as the worst data,
8. Models are not a perfect representation of reality.

Whilst Frank Knight said that uncertainty is separate from risk, he might have meant that uncertainty is not synonymous with risk. Uncertainty lurks inside every part of the development of the risk assessment. We have alluded to some details above, now we need to move on and understand why we struggle to understand risk, because of the limits of both our natural language and our misuse of the mathematical language.

Chapter 2
Misunderstanding Risk

We misunderstand risk not because risk is intrinsically complex, but because we oversimplify the underlying concepts. We are guilty of this both linguistically and mathematically, which is only another language. We need to look at how we muddle the concepts in both of these two channels of communication, not just to misunderstand each other, but to confuse our own understanding.

We use words in a fluid way where the meanings of words become blurred. When this happens the concepts behind each word become obscured and when we attempt to communicate a message about risk it can easily be "lost in translation", even between the experts. Conflict, our Horseman War, is introduced because of the ambiguity that arises in our (mis)understandings.

Another linguistic nuance is the clash between normative analysis and descriptive analysis. A normative analysis is a statement of how things "should be", or a rationalisation, and brings Famine, or subjectivity, into the fray. We confuse it with descriptive analysis where it is reference to a fact, such as a picture being square.

We do something similar with the language of mathematics, where we too narrowly use concepts that have much broader meanings. Here we try and remove 'War' (ambiguity) by restricting the meaning of the mathematical concept. However, we don't remove it, we hide it.

Hiding ambiguity does little more than ensure the answer we appear to have for the risk assessment is wrong. We may feel we have made it clearer but all we have done is donned War's blinkers. We miss the nuance of the risk assessment and hinder our ability to make a rational decision; a subject we'll return to later in the book. Before we get to that we shall look at the way we misunderstand linguistically and mathematically in more detail.

The Language of Risk

This section is an attempt to find our way through the chaos of language, with reference to risk, where meaning changes person by person and shifts subtly depending on context. It is very much an edited highlight of words we use in an imprecise manner rather than a detailed treatise on risk language. Think of it as pointing out the pitfalls we all, experts included, get trapped in sometimes and not a translation guide to a foreign language.

The core of misunderstanding risk is about the "misuse" of words. We say risk when we mean hazard, we say risk when we mean likelihood, or probability. We do this with many words and below we highlight some key ones.

A pivotal misunderstanding in risk assessments is that all outcomes are negative. That is, all things risk assessed are to be avoided. When we make risk assessments about positive things we tend to relate it more to gambling, or project selection. Linguistically we have made risk a negative word, which leaves a void to describe 'gambles' with positive outcomes. What is needed for a general-purpose model based on the one given in Part 1 is a word that encompasses positive and negative outcomes.

Some methods recognise the different potential outcomes, notably the SWOT (Strength-Weakness-Opportunity-Threat) Analysis. Whilst opportunity may convey the positive potential, the use of the word fits in with its counter-part *threat* in the Danger-Impact model, discussed below.

To break the cycle that risk is always negative we can substitute *impact* for *harm*. The principles discussed in Part 1 still stand, but should be reviewed in light of the concept that there may be a positive and/or negative outcome.

If we re-examine the ubiquitous risk matrix (see Figure 2) we can see there is a way to assess the risk of positive and negative impacts together. Care needs to be taken when using the matrix because the tolerance of risk is the same, but what is a good gain is a bad loss. That may seem counter-intuitive at first but a little explanation will make it clear.

Looking at the matrix closely; where the negative impact side is red the positive side is green and vice versa. Imagine you have a sum of money to 'invest'. Small frequent gains would be tolerable, but large frequent gains would be better. Conversely, small frequent losses would be acceptable, but large frequent loses would be intolerable.

Nassim Taleb, in *Black Swan*, suggested that exposure to low frequency high impact positive events, with a low cost, can be an effective strategy to unexpectedly get ahead of the game. Looking at the matrix those would be in the 'green' area of the matrix;

suggesting they are a risk worth taking. However, positive impact assessment is not typically done this way.

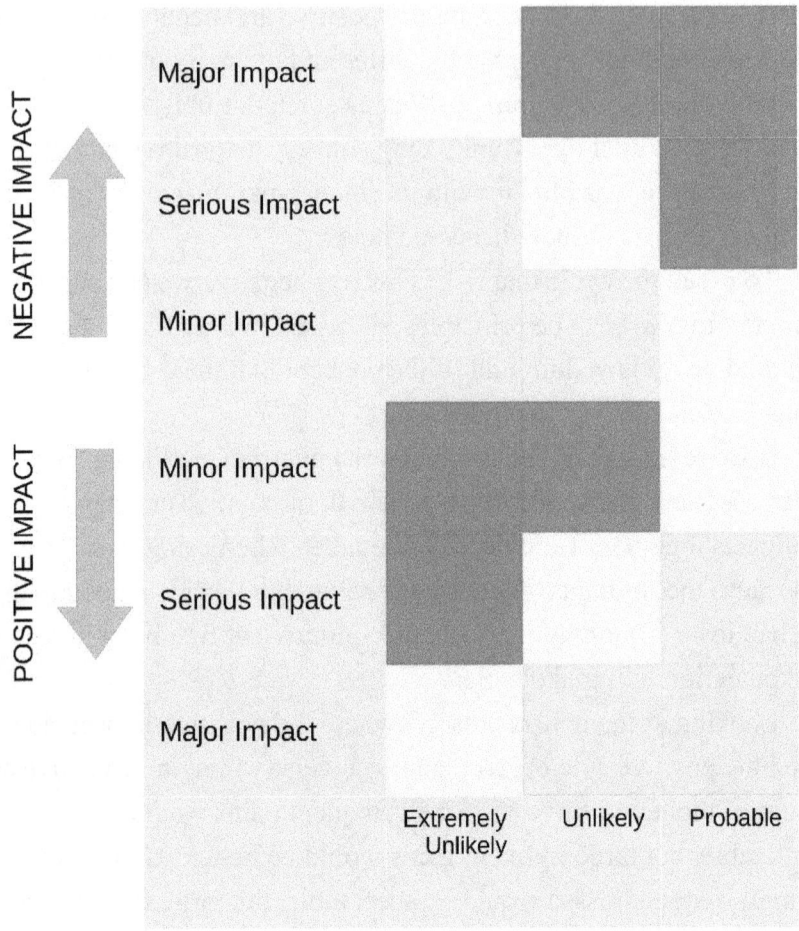

Figure 2 - Risk Matrix

18

Unwittingly most businesses already have a good method for filtering positive impacts. This is the project evaluation process. What is often missed is the language used for it. These evaluations are all about risk, but historically the perception is that it is not a risk assessment. Integrating this into a generic discussion on risk is part of the challenge; the same with many other variations of risk assessments.

To integrate the language of project evaluation, or other process with positive outcomes, we return to review the Danger-Harm Model set out in Part 1. The Danger-Harm model (see Figure 3) places specific words in specific places in the steps of a scenario's timeline. The key elements are re-iterated here and then the model is revised with the inclusion of the equivalent words for a positive impact.

Looking at the words in the order of the model; we start with *danger*. This is something that if 'uncontrolled' can cause an impact. Safety would seem the antonym of danger, but it does not bear the hallmark of latency that danger does. This may be the root of why positive impact assessments are not perceived as a form of risk assessment; i.e. we do not have a positive word with the same emotional content as danger. The struggle is even greater if you look for a word that is neutral, with both negative and positive implications.

Threats are things, or events, that can cause the danger to become 'out of control'; or cause a 'loss of control'. They are many and varied; for example, a wall is a threat to a car driving down the road. As noted above opportunity can be mentally substituted here if the outcome is positive. Again, we seem to lack in our linguistic databanks a word that carries the positive connotations that threat has.

19

Hazards are synonymous with benefits and *harm* equates to gain for the positive version. The nuance between a benefit and a gain
is that a benefit has not been realised by a specific *receptor* whereby it would become a gain. The struggle to find words that carry purely neutral meanings is just as significant here as with all other elements of the model.

The negative risk reducing layers of *prevention, protection, mitigation,* and *vulnerability* do not have obvious linguistic antonyms. Again, this is more likely a reflection of our cultural definition of risk and how we have developed words that fit our need. In Figure 4 I have made some suggestions, but there is still a need to fill this linguistic gap to allow us to communicate risk in a neutral way.

This brief examination of the language around positive and negative risk assessments is about being able to view risk in a bigger sense, not just a negative. The hope is that this is a seed for discussion such that risk language can become unified, rather than just negatively focussed. Without a solid common language we will continue to miscommunicate.

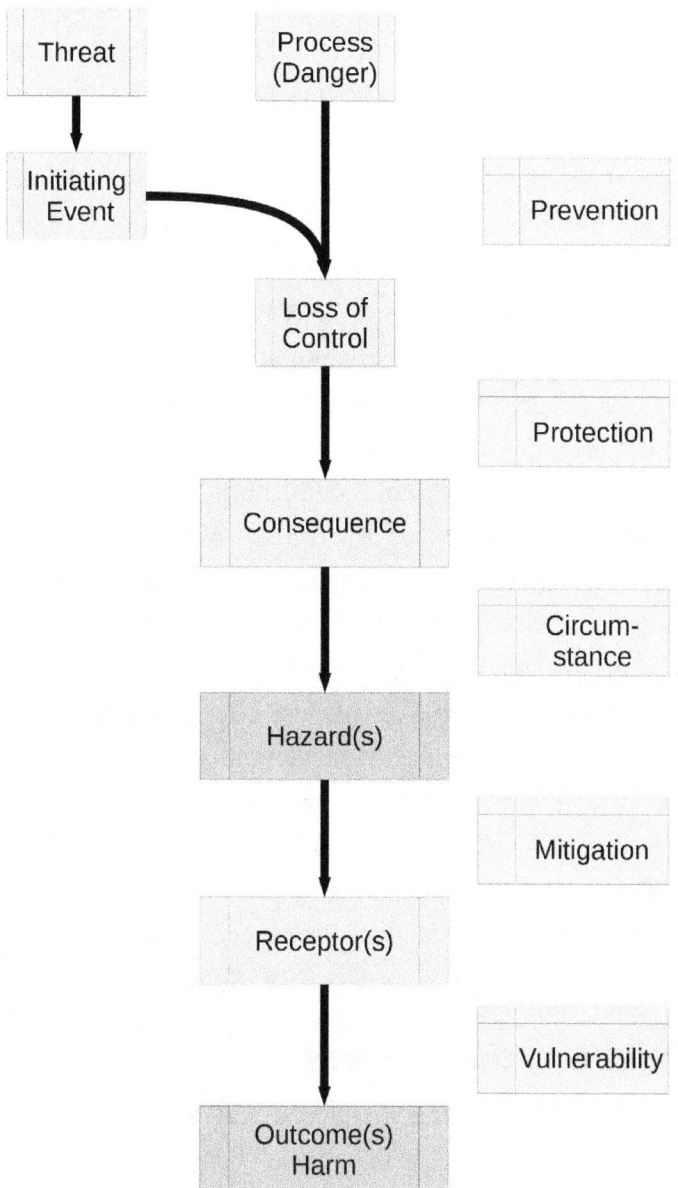

Figure 3 - Danger - Harm Model

The Mathematics of Risk

I am deeply indebted to Terje Aven for his book Misconceptions of Risk which gives a fantastically sound mathematical explanation of the concepts discussed here. However, here I will do him a disservice and present the issues he covers as axioms without the proof that he supplies. If you doubt anything said here, read his book.

In avoiding the use of equations many of the issues raised here may seem more about linguistics than mathematics. However, the truth is that the failing is in our inability to describe the mathematical principle. Whichever perspective you take the underlying issue is a matter of communication and demonstrates the blur between normative and descriptive analysis.

The misunderstandings are grouped into four types. The order is not the same as in Misconceptions of Risk, rather in 'philosophical' groups; however, they are all interconnected. An awareness of them all will make your use of risk assessments very much more powerful. The lack of mathematical formulae only re-emphasises how much our treatment of the principles is a matter of communication, or language, than pure numbers. Although you will think the next section is about normative or linguistic issues, it is not; it is about misunderstanding the objective issues.

Oversimplifying the Numbers

The first oversimplification we have already discussed, and that is the perception that all risk is negative. Thus, because our culture treats risk as negative we believe all the values of risk are negative. This is generally because we see risk as trading off a cost to avoid a possible loss but ignore trading off a cost for a potential gain.

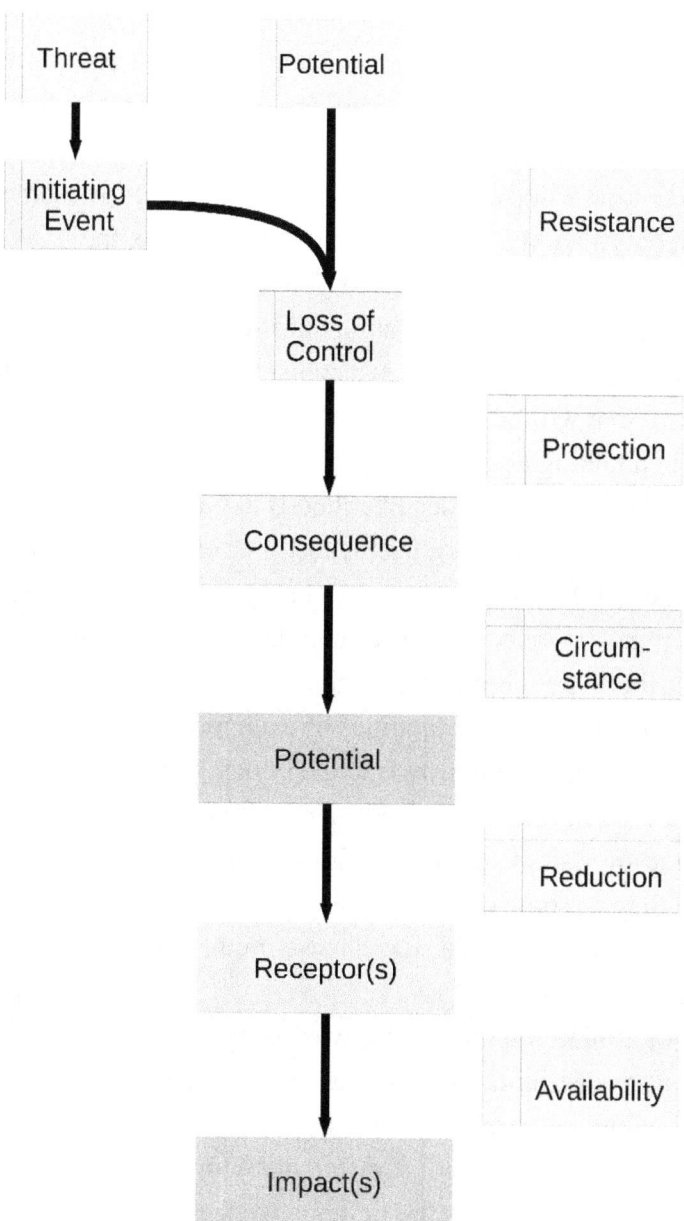

Figure 4 - Potential - Impact Model

The mathematical language is the same, just the answer looks different.

In a similar vein, risk is not the expected dis-utility; dis-utility being the loss experienced from either the outcome, or avoiding the outcome. Famine lurks here and there is a subjective assessment of the value of the dis-utility experienced; for example, the use of the Value of a Statistical Life to standardise the monetary value of an investment to avoid a fatality. However, are all lives of equal value? That is not a question I aim to answer, rather it is to point out that there is a subjective assessment of the type of harm that will be caused.

Even when talking about risk in just its negative form we take the *expected value* (harm times likelihood) to be a fixed single value, which is to miss seeing Pestilence. For example, we may state that the risk for that process is 1 fatality per 100,000 years. However, risk is more complicated than that and is fact the product of two distributions. The *hazard* behind this example may result in no fatality, one fatality, two fatalities or even more. There is a chance it may happen tomorrow and every day until the end of time such that it never happens. Rather than a single value on a page or plotting a single point on a risk matrix we should be putting a circle or some other type of 'blob' on the chart; or showing a distribution. This suggests we might not be certain what the risk really is.

If we plot a 'blob' on the matrix, what is its shape? That depends on the distributions we use to measure harm and likelihood. Our first response is to use a Gaussian type bell curve. It's the distribution we all feel comfortable with when we talk about statistics, because it is the first one we learn. In Black Swan Nassim Taleb argues strongly for the use of Power Law distributions, which give rise to 'long tail' behaviour. These two are not the only options; the log-normal distribution is applicable in many cases, as are a host of other curves. At this point it is unclear whether, War, Pestilence or Famine is at work; or perhaps all three.

There is a small body of work by John Hollman in connection with the *Association for the Advancement of Cost Engineering* (AACE International) that both supports the log-normal type distribution, and even suggests that there may be a more complicated nature underlying processes where a system may exhibit behaviour under one type of distribution but factors may cause the distribution shape to change. This reinforces the lack of certainty we have in what the 'real' risk might be. This is most definitely Pestilence's complexity coming to the fore.

Irrespective of which distribution you choose to represent the likelihood or harm we are making one large assumption. Simply we are assuming that we are taking a sample from a large population and that we can apply 'continuous' statistical analysis. What if we are not working with a sample form a large population? How can we describe the risk? Famine's subtle hand of subjectivity creeps in through our assumption.

Misrepresenting the Numbers

The misrepresentation of risk is, in many ways, an extension of the oversimplification of the numbers. Perhaps this section should be more accurately described as "how to misrepresent the numbers a little less".

Putting blobs on a risk matrix seems an inelegant solution to this issue. Some would argue that methods such, as *total value at risk (TVaR)*, address the blob issue of the risk matrix. TvaR, or sometimes just VaR, is a method that indicates what percentage

25

chance there is of loss, greater than a specified value within a defined time period. It is more commonly used in financial institutions, and is useful when looking at gains and losses. However, it does not reflect the shape of the loss curve, so two 'investments' may have the same TvaR, but one may run the likelihood of a much higher loss.

The assumption that underpins the TvaR type methods is the risk distribution is identical in all cases. Understanding why we misunderstand the nature of the distribution will clarify why these methods do not answer the issues, and still leave the Horseman riding loose in the numbers.

Continuing from where we left off above; our choice of distribution hides the uncertainty we have in the underlying data, be that the complexity of Pestilence or the ambiguity of War. Whatever distribution we choose it is an estimate of reality. This is compounded because we have assumed that all unknown data fits our choice based on the limited dataset we have.

Where do we typically get these limited datasets? The most common way is to collect historical data. This seems a rational starting point, but is fraught with the danger that if we collect data from a series of different distributions and add them together, the Central Limit Theorem states they will develop the characteristics of a normal (Gaussian) distribution. In essence we could be forcing the error of a Gaussian distribution because we have assumed our source data is all part of the same 'population'; we replace Pestilence and War with Famine's subjectivity. The assumptions in the collection and compilation of data may be giving rise to uncertainty, or misrepresentation, in the results, as well.

Combining various risks, with their different distributions, to give an overall risk distribution can be done using the *Monte Carlo* method. This approach allows the potential for all sorts of distributions at the base level, and can result in unusually shaped distributions. This is especially true if events can have alternate distributions dependent on other conditions, as identified by John Hollman.

However, if we give a single curve output from a *Monte Carlo* analysis then we are, again, oversimplifying the issue. Running multiple versions can be informative, but does not address the uncertainty in the underlying data. To tackle that *sensitivity analysis* can be used by repeating the *Monte Carlo* with different values and distributions to assess the change in the risk profile. Although our effort may reduce the uncertainty, it largely becomes an exercise in trading War's ambiguity and Famine's subjectivity for Pestilence's complexity.

To produce multiple Monte Carlo simulations with companion sensitivity analysis can be a burdensome effort. To be sure that the effort is worthwhile, we need to understand the answer that is generated. The sensitivity analysis has shown us where we are least certain we "know" things, but do we know what that lack of knowledge means?

So far it would seem that all that is needed is a better understanding of the mathematical principles and assumptions underlying the risk calculation. Were it that life was so simple; and we will go on to see that it isn't.

Not Being Sure of the Answer

We have developed a comprehensive answer, but how confident are we that we are looking at a reflection of reality? How much uncertainty in our answer? How do we work at eliminating this uncertainty?

We have already conducted sensitivity analysis, and what does this show us? The analysis has not reduced uncertainty; rather it has shown us where uncertainty is highest and where we should expend effort to reduce it. In some cases this is futile and leads to the 'tail wagging the dog'.

Before we proceed it is worth clarifying that the uncertainty is NOT the risk. What we are uncertain about is the accuracy of the answer. The sources of our uncertainty are varied. Examining these sources should help us better understand our confidence, or lack of it, in the answer for risk we calculate.

The first myth to dispel is that the risk assessment creates uncertainty. There is a mathematical axiom that states the accuracy of your answer is only as good as the worst data. If we have poor input data then the output will be poor. The sensitivity analysis can help identify the influence the data quality has, but the data is still the source of uncertainty.

Whilst appearing to contradict the previous paragraph; there is aleatory error in the calculation due to simplification. What this means is that to calculate the risk we have used a model. The model is not reality, but something that provides useful output without excessive effort. Every model is a simplification and this does introduce some uncertainty in whether or not the answer is a reflection of what will happen. The uncertain in a model does not need to be quantified. If its use does not prove useful in making decisions then it should be modified or abandoned.

The choice of model and of base data is done by a person. That person's experience will influence their choices; they will preselect data sources leading to Famine's hand of subjectivity. This influences the uncertainty in the answer.

There are times when the assessor may need to select analogous data because none exists for the issue in question; and so enters either Famine's subjectivity or War's ambiguity. How do we measure the uncertainty of that data? Not everything the assessor uses is objective data, some subjective input is inevitable.

Updating models with Bayesian methods does not improve the answer in all cases. It can be used to improve objective data, but this is only a small part of the issue. Any subjective elements will still remain.

In short, we suffer from epistemic uncertainty, which arises from a lack of (perfect) knowledge leaving us uncertain. Just remember for now that there is uncertainty in the quality/accuracy of the objective data; uncertainty in the subjective assumptions the assessor makes, and aleatory uncertainty from the model used.

Not Understanding the Answer

So far we seemed to have concentrated on making the answer more complicated letting Pestilence creep in, as perhaps it is harder to identify or easier to ignore. So, do our Monte Carlo analyses with sensitivity analysis ensure that we have at last revealed the truth? The short answer is, no. As that stands in direct contradiction to our efforts we need to explore why after all that effort a risk assessment does not reveal "the truth".

Why does our hard-sought number not represent the truth? It is because the attitude to risk is, at its core, a moral or ethical question. The question is not just mathematical, but whether we feel the potential loss is tolerable considering the benefits received. The key question boils down to, "Do I think it is worth it?"

That simple question has two key twists to it that form the root of many business, personal, political, and social questions. The first aspect asks, is the risk tolerable? The second is the perception of the risk. We need to examine both of these in more detail to understand why they create the bedlam that underpins risk based decision making.

How do we define tolerability? Something that is tolerable may not be acceptable. The use of these two concepts as synonyms can create a gap when trying to understand another person's perspective. Simplistically, something is acceptable if the loss or cost is so low that it would be imperceptible to the person facing the risk. It would be tolerable if the reward for facing the risk, even passively, outweighs significantly the cost or potential loss.

That leads us on to the issue of risk perception. Wherever there is a disagreement about the impact or likelihood distributions then perceptions will be different. No party is absolutely certain of its data, however confident. This uncertainty, and differences in it, gives rise to a difference in a perception of the risk.

A factor in the difference in risk perception is because as humans we have, what are known as, cognitive biases. We look at these biases in detail in the next chapter, but accept that we have our own personal experiences that we use to filter the information we receive. If we have taken only one car journey and that involved a crash, we might perceive travel by car as riskier than someone who has never experienced a crash. No amount of hard numbers is likely to change that perception.

Combine the two, different distributions of harm and likelihood with our biases, and you have the issue of the difference in perception of what is a tolerable risk. In Part 1 we discussed how the risk of death in a car crash is often used for defining a value for risk of death from other activities. While this may seem an effective choice of baseline, we return to the issue of the perceived benefits. When defining the *Value of a Statistical Life* the focus is on the economic benefit of the person. When an individual assesses the benefits of driving it includes an array of social and emotional connotations not generally considered in a risk assessment. Thus, while we might see two activities with equal monetary value the person at risk, or even an interested third party, might include an array of other factors that less readily fit into risk analysis.

In the end we have a number, or distribution, we believe is a facsimile of the truth, but someone else can perceive this as a distortion and possibly even an outright lie. As difficult as it may be, we can only address these issues if we walk a mile in the other man's moccasins.

Later in this book we will examine how, despite all this, we still manage to make effective decisions. Having said that, those decisions are still rooted in the decision makers risk perception, which may be very different from others that feel the impact of that decision.

Chapter 3
Cognitive Biases

Human beings do not process data or make decisions in a logical manner; or make a pure normative analysis. Humans use a number of models that are a form of descriptive analysis that have been shown to result in rational, but not logical decisions. The nuance used here is that rational can be explained, but logic is objective; and we noted above that risk assessments are not wholly objective. This subtle difference can be hard to follow, but logic is based solely on validated data; whereas rational arguments can be based on experience and reasoning with a lower level of 'proof' required on the constituent parts.

The need for large amounts of human mental input in the generation of scenarios (see Part 1), or the stories that lead to an Outcome, and the inevitable selection of numerical data, models and subjective assessments means we cannot ignore the decision making process and the role biases can play in distorting them.

There are two camps in psychology that take epistemologically opposed perspectives on why there is a difference between how humans make rational decisions versus a benchmark of 'pure logic'. One school, ecological rationality, looks at the strategies the people use to make effective decisions under uncertainty. The other school looks at the biases humans have as deviations from purely logical decisions; assumed to be under perfect information. As always there are ardent supporters of both camps, which are really opposite sides of the same coin and there is value in looking at issues from both perspectives.

Both schools use the principle of heuristics to explain the simplified mental processes humans use to arrive at conclusions. For ecological rationality these exist because they are an effective means of conserving effort and achieving an answer that is better than most other 'complex' selection methods; especially with uncertain data. For the cognitive bias school the heuristic causes us to make a sub-optimal decision, which can be explained as a bias away from the decision that would be made if there was no uncertainty.

For now we shall see how these biases are the doors through which the Four Horsemen ride. Sometimes the doors are open so wide that they are hidden in plain sight and the Horsemen enter all too easily. In Chapter 5 we will return to look at the flip side of the coin and see how we make decisions that allow us to avoid the Four Horseman more often than would seem statistically fair.

Bias, What Bias?

Before we discuss heuristics, we will glance at some specific biases. Biases are more readily recognised because they are often noticed when there is a difference in the level of knowledge (certainty of data) between two people. When we are in the position of greater knowledge, then seeing the other person's bias is comparatively easy.

There are extensive lists of *cognitive biases* and an excellent summary work of most of these is Daniel Kahneman's *Thinking Fast and Slow*. Table 1- Decision Making Biases, Table 2- Social biases, and Table 3 - Probability & Belief biases at the end of the chapter include lists of some of those biases with a brief explanation of what they mean. There are many more, and they may all have some indication on our deviation from a perfectly logic risk assessment. These cover every step from the scenario generation (see Part 1) to the selection of data to generate the risk profile.

The reader's challenge is to see how the heuristics we discuss below lead to those biases. Taking a page from ecological rationality the resultant bias will depend on the context that the conclusion was drawn in. The myriad of interconnections you should see explains the difficult in the areas of human behaviour.

Start as You Mean to Go on

Heuristics is an area of study that dates back to early work on problem solving. Identifying risks is a form of problem solving, so we can be confident that whatever issues are thrown up by heuristics will apply to risk assessments. Therefore, we should take a brief look at their history and the key types of heuristic.

Heuristics have been with humanity since the dawn of time. They are often summed up as *rules of thumb* and maybe even *common sense*. Both of those are gross oversimplifications of what heuristics really are. Although they're both included, they are a tiny subset of heuristics. In short, every mental model we have is a heuristic.

Even the way we kick or throw a ball, hit moving objects, drive, interact with other people are all heuristics. These are mental models we use to filter the world and our interaction with it. They are *constructs*, or cognitive maps that we use to interpret the world and the data we receive from it [Fish, a].

What has happened over the intervening years is that generalisations of mental models have been developed, and these are the *psychological heuristics* of today. It is at this point that the two divergent perspectives on heuristics starts. Of the two schools of thought we will follow the one associated with Kahneman for the remainder of this chapter.

The reason for following Kahneman is because we are going to take the assumption used by that school, which is that we are intending to make decisions based on a complete set of information; without uncertainty and in a totally logic manner. Kahneman and Tversky referred to the "people" that made these 'perfect logical' decisions as *econs*. Remember the assumption of comparison of people's decisions with those of *econs*, it is key to the way we view heuristics and biases; paraphrasing Eli Goldratt in *The Goal*, that if the model is no longer working then the issue is the assumptions you are using.

The Three Kings

Daniel Kahneman and Amos Tversky published an article in *Science* in 1974 entitled *Judgement under Uncertainty: Heuristics and Biases*. In this they set out the three core heuristics that believe people use when making assessments about probability; which is another way of saying; risk assessment. These three are called:

1. Representativeness;
2. Availability; and
3. Adjustment & Anchoring.

These heuristics give rise to biases away from a decision made by perfect knowledge. They are the short cuts we use to make up for the uncertainty in the available data. The article, which is available on the web, or better yet the book *Thinking, Fast and Slow*, expands on these and has the original article included in an appendix, but we will summarise them here.

They are discussed in a different order here than in the original paper, but only to demonstrate the order they are likely to be experienced when carrying out a risk assessment. We will, also, look at how these influence our interpretation of the risk. However, the examination of the influence of these biases is only light here, as we return to these issues in a later chapter.

Availability

When we start a risk assessment and are generating scenarios by assessing threats and evaluating hazards we are often subconsciously filtering our answers, or whether we believe some kind of associated event is credible. If we cannot readily recall similar types of event, then we may ignore potential hazards. Equally, if we can readily recall an instance, perhaps one that has been in the news or has happened recently on our facility then we may over emphasise it. We fill the Famine of objective data with subjective data.

This *bias of retrievable instances* causes us to believe that events are more probable than they may be. It creates an expectation of the risk that is purely subjective. This is why scenario generation and likelihood judgements are best separated in the sequence. This is particularly true after some type of mishap has occurred, where we believe that these rare events are more common than objective data would suggest.

This retrievability bias is closely related to our ability to recall similar events that have some strong connection in the sequence of events leading to the scenario, or have some other common feature, such as the type of equipment being studied. If what we are examining is short on those 'common features' then we may be less willing to entertain the credibility of those events.

One strength of most scenario generation methods is that they directly address the threshold of mental effort required to imagine an event. Our ability to imagine an event is essential to being able to risk assess it, although this is a double-edged sword.

When we can imagine these scenarios we can develop a belief that more frequent events are prevented more often than they are because we can readily imagine them being avoided. However, having created a scenario of a previously unforeseen event we believe it is much more likely than data might suggest. This is a variation of the *narrative fallacy* that Nassim Taleb discusses in *Black Swan*. Just because we can readily imagine a sequence of events, and thus create a plausible story / narrative does not influence the likelihood of it occurring.

However, just because we can imagine an event does not mean that we can directly draw background data about it. We may not have experience, even second-hand, that relates to it. To bridge that gap we look for something that can *represent* those events, as analogies.

Representativeness

When we are faced with something we don't know, or where there is uncertainty we rephrase the question such that it is about something that we do know. This can happen consciously or subconsciously, but it happens either way. What we are asking ourselves when we do this is, "Is this other thing B representative of the problem, A, that I am dealing with now?" Here, War prances in as we introduce ambiguity by creating a new question rather than answering the original one.

The guiding principle here is that every analogy breaks down at some point. There are numerous examples of how this 'nearly the same' heuristic works very well. Equally, there are times when the approach breaks down. When asked if they were an above average driver, 80% of people replied that they were. Defining an average driver is difficult, but the respondents rephrased the question to themselves along a single dimension that reflected well on their driving ability. Perhaps more surprising is the honesty of the remaining 15%. There is little point citing more examples as I am sure you will either think of, or experience many in the next few hours.

Unfortunately, this analogy approach hides many useful elements of data from our thought processes. The example Kahneman and Tversky use is about being given partial information about a person that causes us to categorise them as a librarian. In their studies they showed that this analogy approach causes us to ignore what they refer to as *prior probability*. In short because the limited data available suggests a certain analogy we tend to use that analogy (or subset of data) rather than consider a more common subset of data is applicable.

In process industry assessments, for example *API581 Reliability Based Inspection*, failure data is modified based on the nature of the environment. There are descriptions of what these environments are like and these can cause us to incorrectly associate the conditions we are assessing, because we select the 'wrong' analogous data.

Another aspect of our belief in the strength of our chosen analogy is that we believe that the chosen data is valid. This is true irrespective of the quality, or reliability, of the data we are using to make our assumption of analogy. Once we have chosen the analogy we are convinced that all subsequent inferences are valid. This can lead us to be overconfident in the final assessment without consideration to the quality of input data.

This *illusion of validity* is related to our tendency to establish a mental baseline from the first data we associate with an event. We see this in everyday life in events as trivial as knowing what someone else paid for an item, or what we have paid in the past, and our expectation is to pay a similar amount. Kahneman and Tversky referred to this as *anchoring*.

Adjustment & Anchoring

As we noted above, we tend to start with some value fixed in our head when looking at probabilities. What is most disconcerting about this is the number of sources that can influence this *anchor*. We mentioned the use of incorrect analogy data above, but we can be influenced by values in a previous, totally unrelated conversation or experience.

We do not blindly follow these anchors, what happens is that we make insufficient *adjustment* to the value to reflect the current situation. People that are seeded with an *anchor* of a low number underestimate and those seeded with a high number over estimate; even if all other information available is identical.

This is connected with our tendency to link our estimate with a probability distribution. When we have a low anchor we move upwards based on an assumed *subjective probability distribution* and downwards using the same distribution if we know we are anchored high. Our errors tend to arise because we are using the wrong distribution when we make the adjustment.

Unless we have an experience that establishes a different choice of distribution we default to some form of simple symmetrical distribution. Figure 5 shows simple square section, triangular, and normal/Gaussian distribution. These are *anchors* in our experience and education systems. This is because we tend to follow the route of least mental effort; Kahneman's *System 1*, or fast, thinking. Thus, unless we are explicitly externalising this in a calculation we are likely to use a simplified assumption of the distribution shape. Completely avoiding our notice Pestilence has infected our thinking because we have not noted the complexity in the system, by making simplifying assumptions to minimise our mental effort.

If we are all prone to these simple biases then it would seem a simple case of providing an offset to balance them. Unfortunately, the real world is more complex than that. We are subject to other influences that alter our perceptions, and cause us to ignore or invite in one of the Horsemen to our risk assessment and decision making process.

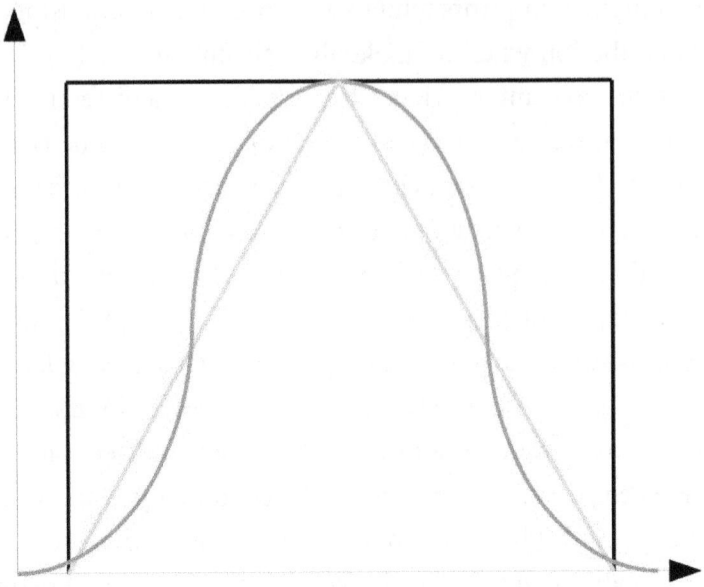

Figure 5- Symmetrical Distributions

Framing and Other Influences

What I have grouped as the *Three Kings* of availability, representativeness and anchoring do not existing in a vacuum. Every little piece of our personal journey through life will have some influence on how "biased" we are; which explains the difference of opinion between experts when the layman would expect agreement. Herein lies the seeds to every risk assessment being wrong.

While there are a variety of influences on the strength and direction of our biases the largest is how the question is *framed*. This is as simple as it seems and means depending on how we phrase the question will influence what answer we get. That means if the same question is rephrased in a mathematically identical but linguistically different manner, we get a different answer.

Our treatment of risk depends on whether the outcome is framed as a gain or a loss. Our approach to risk is heavily influenced by the perception of certainty; but our attitude to certainty is influenced by whether the outcome is a gain or a loss. In Chapter 4 we shall return to this issue of perceived certainty and here we will look at how we respond to how the question of risk is framed.

We are more likely to respond positively to a 70% chance of success than to a 30% chance of failure. It is simple to see that the two are mathematically equivalent. The point is that we respond to them at an instinctive, or emotional, level rather than what pure logical should suggest; hence we do not react like an *econ*. Although, this has been demonstrated in research experiments, what does not exist is research as to how we respond to subtle modifications to the framing language. Such changes as the use on the word 'only'; for example "only a 70% chance of success"; or at what point do we carry out reverse mental arithmetic and recognise that a 40% chance of success is a sleight of hand to hide a 60% chance of failure. Undoubtedly this is a rich vein for future research.

As we noted our attitude to certainty varies depending on whether or not the outcome is a gain or a loss. When we are likely to gain from a risk, we take certainty in preference to an equal gamble. Because this is a mathematical concept we need to use some numbers to explain this. Suppose we are offered a choice where we can either take $800 or an 80% chance of winning $1,000. Did you notice that you instinctively chose the certain $800? Mathematically the other choice is equal and an *econ* would have no preference either way. Already you are trying to explain your preference, because there is a chance with the gamble that you will get nothing. This is because at an instinctual level we do not make the mistake of thinking that our statistical data is from a "large population"; a mistake we noted in Chapter 2 when we misunderstand the mathematics of risk.

Curiously our approach to risk is reversed when the outcome is a loss. We favour the gamble when the outcome is a loss. Reversing the example above; would you choose to lose $800 or gamble at an 80% chance of losing $1,000? The decision bias here is to accept the gamble. A similar logic is applied as before in that we see a chance to lose nothing; 20% of the time.

Interestingly we respond with the same bias to certainty in both gains and losses, as noted above, even when the other option is clearly a better choice. Simply stated, we prefer a certain gain over a potentially larger, but uncertain gain; and we would choose a larger loss, but with an uncertain potential for a smaller loss, over a certain loss. What is at work here is an emotionally driven *risk aversion*.

So how do we define *risk aversion*? Perhaps the first step is to define *loss aversion*, which is related, but not the same. Loss aversion is our tendency to place greater emotional significance on losing $100 than on gaining $100. This is not a new revelation; as the origins of this date to work by Bernoulli in 1738. Although his work is considerably more sophisticated a rule-of-thumb that can be taken from it is the 2/3rds rule. We value a gain with the same emotion as a loss of 2/3rds of the value. This can be restated in an example that we emotionally equate a loss of $100 with a gain of $150. The value you place on our gains and losses is referred to as psychological utility and is a form of quantifying our emotional value of the money or other item.

This relates back to how we frame the state of the outcome for an event. If the description is stated as a loss, then we will make more effort to avoid it than if it is rephrased as a gain. This example is manufactured to make the point, whereas in reality the phrasing is often more subtle and we miss the very fact that it is being done. You have an investment that will return $50, but it must be processed through one of two potential task regimes. You can take an option that assures you of a $20 return or another that assures you of a $30 loss. Reread that and assure yourself that mathematically both outcomes are the same; you have a net of $20. However, it is likely that you automatically showed a preference for the former, rather than the later.

Now that we've looked at *loss aversion*, what is *risk aversion*? At first glance we can define *risk aversion* without reference to *loss aversion*. *Risk aversion* is our preference to choose an outcome with less uncertainty than choose one that may give a higher benefit, or lower loss, but with an uncertain outcome. This echoes the discussion above about uncertainty, and emphasises our desire for certainty over the mathematical value of the outcome. In essence we want to avoid *Death* in our decisions.

A clear outward example of risk aversion in business is the urge to 'comply with standards'. The knowledge that our process or product complies with a standard removes the uncertainty around it. There is a temptation to suggest that this is more an inability to make decisions, but the reality is that it is about avoiding risk. When we are not the ones that will bear the consequences of an outcome we may make the more logical, but no more rational, choice to take another course of action.

The use of compliance with standards has another 'advantage' in that it converts any perceived loss into costs; which reduces our aversion to taking the risk by creating a sense of pseudo certainty. Again, we take a greater risk because the uncertainty is lower and the outcome is driven by a cost (compliance) rather than the loss (utility lost). These two factors are large psychological drivers behind the creation of standards, and also act as inhibitors to innovation. However, there are reasons why sometimes outsiders rise to challenge standards, and the way things are done.

If we all showed the same level of risk aversion then things would be comparatively simple. However, we also measure losses and gains not in absolute terms, but in relative terms. This seems self-evident if we compare how a millionaire feels about a certain $5 and a slim chance of gaining $20; compared to a cashless student. Irrespective of the utility of the $20 gamble the millionaire is more likely to gamble and the student more likely to take the sure thing. Hence, the millionaire may now seem to be contradicting the behaviour patterns we set out above.

Sadly, this is not the end of the distortions we put on risk assessments. There are still a few other mental biases that strongly interfere with our ability to make purely logical risk assessments.

Other Faces of Bias

The biggest single stumbling block with risk assessments that we have not discussed is sometimes referred to as the *bias of imaginability*, or the phrase coined by Nassim Taleb in *Black Swan* is the *narrative fallacy*. The concept is simple and is fundamentally the basis of all the hazard identification tools discussed in Part 1. If we can imagine a narrative, or story, for an event occurring then we feel it is more probable than if we cannot.

You can see this bias in action in two circumstances. The first is during a hazard study where, despite a clear narrative having been developed, members of the group will consider the scenario 'not credible' because prior to this point they had not envisaged the sequence of events. This is often when a scenario involves a large number of 'failures' to occur in sequence; even if the likelihood of these failures, individually, is high.

The second time this occurs is the reverse effect. If a mishap has occurred recently at the facility; often the motive for conducting a hazard/risk review; then people are convinced the likelihood of a similar event is much higher than objective data would indicate because the narrative is much stronger based on recent experience. This often involves a disproportionate response to the risk posed by the scenario. In simple terms, because you have rolled a 5 on a six-sided die does not make it more likely to get 5 on the next roll.

This belief that the scenario is more probable than is estimated because of its recent occurrence is an example of our inability to appreciate the impact of sample size on statistical results. We over emphasise the high likelihood due to the recent mishap, whilst potentially ignoring a large collection of data that contradicts this. This is equally apt to occur when new designs are introduced and are deemed safe or dangerous based on little data, due to little more than good fortune or misfortune from a small sample of data.

This belief that the next roll is more likely to be the same, or that small data samples represent the whole story is closely related to the idea of the illusory correlation. In the 'bias' we connect to small samples of data that have no correlation because of some commonality. For example, a facility has had five mishaps and three occur on Tuesdays. It is possible to infer that a mishap is more likely on a Tuesday. Whilst this conclusion may have a basis in truth, it is likely that it is an *illusory correlation*.

While we often make connections where there are none, we are also poor at comprehending the difference in likelihood between *conjunctive* and *disjunctive* scenarios. *Conjunctive* scenarios are ones where there are events that occur together; A <u>and</u> B happen,

47

usually in sequence; and many risk analysis tools are well equipped to handle this scenario.

Disjunctive scenarios are more complex and situations where A occurs on its own, or B occurs on its own, or A and B occur together. This type of scenario can lead to complex representations, especially if there are multiple disjunctive elements to a scenario, and most existing tools do not provide a way to present this clearly. In all cases the human mind typically poorly handles the mathematics, even with training in statistics. This often leads to a disbelief in the likelihood of scenarios that include disjunctive elements. These are the times we ignore Pestilence and the way complexity infects the process.

Perhaps the one we are all most familiar with is called *motivated reasoning*. Simply; if you are to gain from a decision going a certain way you will confabulate every reason to push the result towards what we want, and discredit or ignore any evidence or uncertainty that would push it away from the one we want.

The final bias, or self-deception, we will examine is the tendency to use *regression to the mean*. The natural human tendency to use averages rather than ranges is referred to as *regression to the mean*. This is compounded by the presentation of objective data collected on failures to be presented as the averages; the use of terms such as *mean time between failures* (MTBF) and other terms that imply a single failure frequency. This tends to create the belief in a single point of failure; for example, if an outcome is given a likelihood of once every 300 years we read this that the event will not occur for 300 years. This ignores the potential for the event to occur the following day or not for thousands of years.

Summary

This chapter has been a roller-coaster review of various psychological factors that influence our preparation and interpretation of risk assessments. We have only covered the ones that in my opinion are most significant when preparing and interpreting risk assessments.

Although we address Famine's subjectivity with our imagination, and War's ambiguity with unjustified confidence, a key theme to note is that these biases are dominated by our tendency to ignore complexity; the Pestilence that rots away at our ability to comprehend the totality of the risk assessment. This is more likely a reflection of our brains' inability to process such complex, and potentially chaotic models where we tend to use ones that are "good enough"; something we return to when we look at decision making. Below is a short recap that provides some clarity to the messy interconnectedness of these biases.

The *Three Kings* of availability, representativeness, and adjustment & anchoring are present when we are imagining scenarios and preparing likelihood estimates for risk assessments. They can cause the very foundations of the risk assessment to be wrong. How can we expect good decisions if the information presented has been distorted, unintentionally, in its preparation?

Even if the information of the risk has been presented without distortion by the influence of the Three Kings we have to fight a complex set of inter-related biases. Do we see the outcome as a loss, cost, or gain? Do we select a sure thing over another with higher uncertainty, and is that altered by our perception of gains and losses? Do various parties have different reference points that alter their perspective of loss and redefine their loss-aversion? Has this myriad of inter-related biases been triggered by how the risk has been framed? While it is impossible to eliminate these biases it is possible to restate the information and mentally adopt a different reference point. These take effort and involve engaging *System 2*, which means they are unlikely to be used as often as they should.

We touched on a few other biases, that are key to muddling risk assessments, but there is a long and extensive list of biases. The biases of reducing the sense of likelihood due to *imaginability*, or *illusionary correlations* is compounded by under estimating likelihood because of complex, *disjunctive*, scenarios or our tendency to use *regression to the mean* to create a single point of failure rather accepting the breadth of failure potential.

Being handicapped by these biases may seem bad enough, but there are times when we are more vulnerable to the biases and other mistakes. The factors influencing our susceptibility to greater biases are mostly covered by Human Error and are the subject of the next chapter.

Table 1- Decision Making Biases

Name	Description
Endowment effect	the fact that people often demand much more to give up an object than they would be willing to pay to acquire it
Framing	drawing different conclusions from the same information, depending on how that information is presented
Loss aversion	the disutility of giving up an object is greater than the utility associated with acquiring it
Pseudo certainty effect	the tendency to make risk-averse choices if the expected outcome is positive, but make risk-seeking choices to avoid negative outcomes

Table 2- Social biases

Name	Description
Dunning-Kruger effect	when people are incompetent in the strategies they adopt to achieve success and satisfaction, they suffer a dual burden: Not only do they reach erroneous conclusions and make unfortunate choices, but their incompetence robs them of the ability to realize it. Instead, ...they are left with the mistaken impression that they are doing just fine

Table 3 - Probability & Belief biases

Name	Description
Anchoring	the tendency to rely too heavily, or "anchor," on a past reference or on one trait or piece of information when making decisions
Availability heuristic	a biased prediction, due to the tendency to focus on the most salient and emotionally-charged outcome
Conjunction fallacy	the tendency to assume that specific conditions are more probable than general ones
Recency effect	the tendency to weigh recent events more than earlier events
Subadditivity effect	the tendency to judge probability of the whole to be less than the probabilities of the parts

Chapter 4
Human Error

It is bad enough that we have innate mental models that cause us to deviate from the truly logical approach/solution, but we are also hindered by the potential for genuine human errors. These are not heuristics but genuine errors in the processing of information; which can lead to errors in action. These are when the correct data goes in, but is incorrectly processed and we take the wrong action.

Human beings are prone to mistakes. They are an essential part of progress; just think that every time you choose to do something differently it is a 'mistake', and those may be the positive ones. However, the positive ones are more intriguing because humans generally follow the Law of Least Effort, which is a fancy way of saying we are lazy.

This is where we return to Daniel Khaneman's school of psychology and the book *Thinking Fast & Slow*. Khaneman postulates that the human mind has two 'thinking systems'. There is System 1 which is fast and efficient in terms of mental effort, but uses very simple rules to function. The other is System 2, which is effective and requires significant effort to engage and analyses new experiences and situations, where we cannot immediately apply prior experience. System 1 is prone to biases and both systems are prone to errors. These are not physically identifiable parts of the brain, rather they are diffuse interactions of the subsystems of the brain [Fish, a]

In the first instance we should examine the kind of errors that people make. The groupings are broad and intended to apply to every form of human endeavour. There are three broad categories:

1. Deviation;
2. Inattention; and
3. Lack of Capability.

These are categories that cover many sins. To better understand how all human error is covered by these categories we shall look at more readily identifiable examples.

Deviation covers the acts of doing something that is a *violation* of the intended procedure. This is a deliberate act and includes both invention and sabotage. Both are driven by a decision to do something other than what is intended, but generally the motives are different. This category stretches our original definition of human error because the implication that incorrect processing is the error, rather than deliberate action. The issue of sabotage is beyond the scope of this book, and invention and innovation is a whole subject area in its own right [Fish (b)].

However, a *deviation* also covers doing the wrong thing for the right reasons. A harmless example would be taking the turning to go home after work, rather than take a different route to the meeting you have planned. Simply, the brain believes it is doing the right thing (process) and on many occasions this is fine, however, there are occasions when it has led to disaster.

Inattention blurs with the latter type of deviation. In this case the data is incorrectly processed by System 1, which results in the wrong next step being taken. This covers most actions seen as human error and covers everything from misreading a signpost and taking a wrong turning, to correctly isolating a dangerous system and then working on the near identical live one. Examples are plentiful and there is no need to look for more here.

Lack of capability may not at first seem like human error, so we need to give it some context. If you can't juggle then you don't start with chainsaws. That is a deliberately absurd example to make a point. There are actions we can clearly comprehend that we lack the prerequisite abilities to complete. Attempting these actions could be considered a deviation, but the subtle difference of our inability to complete the correct outcome makes these their own category.

Deviations are wilful acts and are not discussed further here. The case for this is that these are not *errors* in the sense of mishaps; rather the outcome is intended to be different from the norm. That leaves *Inattention* and *lack of capability* to examine in more detail, notably what causes us to be more susceptible to them.

Inattention

Inattention is generally driven by two factors; fatigue or mental overload, often called cognitive dissonance. Fatigue is easy to understand, and *cognitive dissonance* is a state where a person holds conflicting mental concepts that leave them unclear as to what choice to make, or action for follow. However, we will examine both in more detail for clarity.

Fatigue is a surprisingly broad subject. We are interested in issues that result in a tendency to rely on *System 1* for easy answers, and do not engage *System 2* to make more considered decisions. Causing people, by design, to use System 2 is a violation of the "Law of Laziness", which states that people will attempt to expend as little energy as possible to achieve an objective. While we may frequently complain about people's lack of effort this "law" is also the route to innovation as people are inspired to find easier ways to do things; less effort in the future by trading of effort now. Innovation is the subject of another book [ref Fish (b)], so here we will concentrate on the causes of mistakes.

Although physical tiredness is the first type of fatigue that will come to mind, there are many others that can manifest themselves as acute or chronic mental fatigue. Mental fatigue can arise from things as varied as dealing with complex processes or high levels of novelty, where *System 2* has heavily used in the immediate past. A variation of this is dealing with a poorly designed process; which to the developer may seem simple or obvious but requires the user to make a high number of 'novel' decisions.

More difficult to identify are external fatigue factors that can lead to both acute and chronic fatigue. In most management text books these factors are related to stress, and in safety texts they are often referred to as *performance influencing factors*. Stress is a subject matter in its own right, although it is touched upon in two other books in this collection [Fish(a), Fish(c)].

One commonly unseen factor is the process complexity. This can be one of two things. It can be a complicated sequence of steps, perhaps conditional on results as the process progresses, difficult to retain in memory. Alternatively, the process could show complex behaviour, where the response of the process to external stimulus/control is dependent on more variables than can readily be understood. In the latter case the process may not respond as expected, when there is an effort to correct a deviation causing the process to appear/become uncontrollable. This tends not to be a problem in the preparation of risk assessments, but may be missed in the analysis of risk related to a process.

Related factors include those in the list below; and are often hard to "see" when preparing a hazard analysis and risk assessment.

1. Insufficient time available to complete the task; which can result in 'shortcuts' being taken.
2. Not providing the correct tool(s);
3. A poor working environment; which raises stress levels and mental fatigue, increasing the likelihood of errors;
4. Pressure to complete work versus ensuring it is done to procedure/safely.

While it is possible to further subdivide the factors that lead to mental fatigue those described above cover them all. Irrespective of their source anything that increases fatigue, or stress, will increase the likelihood of poor decisions.

Lack of Capability

Lack of capability is a much broader and nuanced subject than it first appears based on the previous blunt example. The prime nuance is when we do not realise that we lack the capability due to our overconfidence, or just being asked to do something we are not capable of doing.

The lack of capability can range from the simple sets of physical limitations; including height, strength, etc.; and lack of training. These can be readily identified because they are measurable and often visible. What is harder to measure are the invisible ones.

Skill, training and competence are terms used to describe the ability to execute an action. We have developed testing and record keeping to track these for specific areas. I do not intend to cover these as they are well understood, as well as being a potentially broad subject. If you have a deep interest in these there are many books and guides on subject.

What is of more interest is the unseen that could be described as "the state of mind". This is more subtle than fatigue or stress. These are more closely related to biases and might be best thought of as mental states where we tend to be more prone to bias than at other times.

The first, and in some ways most disconcerting, is for the self-confident person who has a sense of high personal power, typified by the alpha type, but it is possible for any person to tend to become less risk averse or even become risk seeking. This is likely to be a combination of mental transfer of losses to costs and the belief that the likelihood can be directly influenced by their actions, directly or indirectly. This would tend to suggest that those promoted to positions of power are more likely to make *Type 1 errors*[1]. This is a potential explanation for the string of new business failures and the more notable spectacular success of some people.

An interesting situation arises based on the level of confidence a person has relative to their experience. This is known as the *Dunning-Kruger Effect*. In Figure 6 it can be seen there is a period in the early stages (low knowledge and experience), where the

---

[1] A Type 1 error is asserting something that is absent; in the case of a decision it is doing something that should not be done.
A Type 2 error is failing to assert what is present or not doing something that should be done.

confidence in "too high" compared to experience, which then suffers a rapid reversal eventually recovering.

We see this in subtle ways in life in general, a ready example being the confidence that teenagers exude when they drive cars, and this is reflected in accident and fatality statistics for this group. The Dunning-Kruger effect was described by them as, "…unskilled people tend to overestimate their abilities, and skilled people tend to underestimate them." Driving teenagers are a group that are readily identified as 'unskilled', or inexperienced, and this effect suggests there is truth in the belief that teenager drivers are reckless.

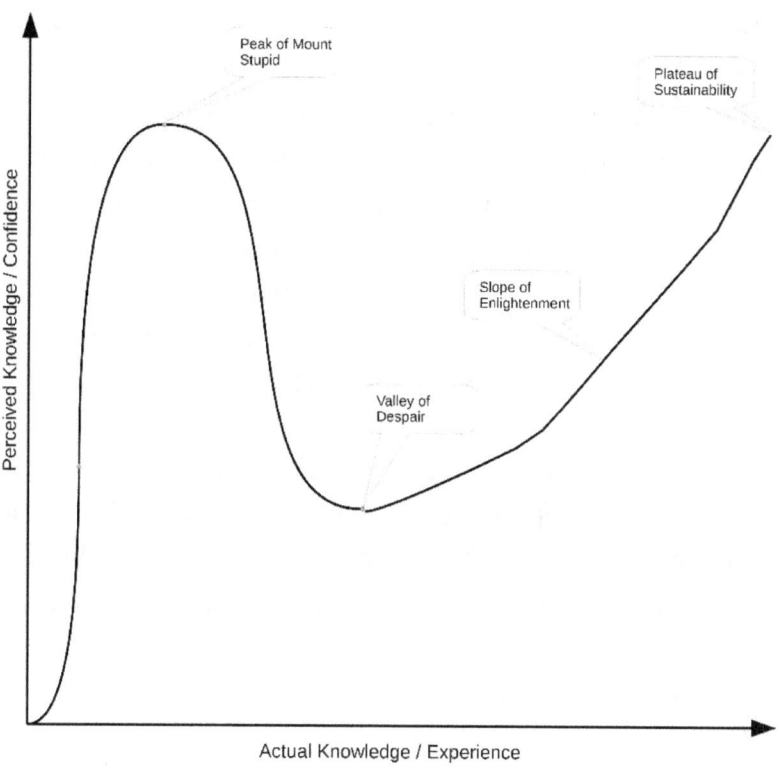

Figure 6 - Dunning-Kruger Effect

It is not just teenagers, or anyone learning a new skill that is vulnerable to this overconfidence. When asked a question that is not easily answered, we substitute a simpler question in our mental process to answer. This is a reiteration of one of the *Three Kings*, *representativeness*, which we saw in previous chapter. When asked in a survey if they are a good driver 80% of people responded that they were above average. Even more illuminating is that 95% of university lecturers in a survey thought that they were above average teachers. It would be easy to write this off as conceit, and whilst we seldom wish to think ill of ourselves, the truth is we substitute a simpler question. This is another example of the *Law of Least Effort* where we engage the rapid *System 1* and avoid the mental effort of using *System 2*.

This substitution does not even have to be about ourselves. We use it when asked about uncertain subjects. When asked if there is data for a type of equipment and there is not, we may justify the values used by substituting analogous equipment data. This is not a poor method, but we must recognise the uncertainty that is introduced. As we noted in the previous chapter, the Horsemen can enter in all their guises and this overconfidence makes it harder for us to see.

A combination of the Dunning-Kruger Effect and substitution may result in 'the top experts', making predictions in the media that are far less accurate than those of the 'industry average expert'. There are other factors at play, but it does raise questions about the reliance on the more notable experts for accurate inputs or analysis of risk assessments.

Summary

It is difficult to predict the *local rationality* in which a decision will be made under. The factors listed above set the tone for mental state of the people preparing and making decision on risk assessments.

Again, this chapter would seem a rambling discourse about the factors that cause people to be more likely to make poor decisions at all stages of the risk assessment process. The truth is that we cannot avoid these errors and biases; they are an intrinsic part of human nature. These errors are elements of increased uncertainty in the risk assessment.

Summary

Chapter 5
Deciding with Uncertainty

It is all too easy to arrive at this juncture having lost all faith in ability to assess risk, and even more so without any confidence in the more impressive risk assessments we see for hazardous activities; from flying to nuclear meltdowns. Risk assessments, and by inference all decision making, is riddled with uncertainty. Even uncertainty that we can't define is there, the infamous 'unknown unknowns'.

Listen to the talk from politicians and economists about Donald Trump as President and the impact of *Brexit* in early 2017. You will hear the word uncertainty used repeatedly. This returns to the earlier comments about our association of uncertainty with negative impacts. Here the word is being used to express that fear of a negative outcome from the risk.

Look at Jeff Bezos' letter to shareholders of Amazon in 2017. He talks of great leaders being able to make decisions with 70% of the potential information, rather than the more usual 90%. He is encouraging people to make decisions with more uncertainty, but isn't that contrary to everything we discussed about biases and reducing uncertainty? Maybe we should reflect on what uncertainty is and examine how we make decisions, even when "30%" of our data maybe "unknown".

The economist Frank Knight described uncertainty as separate from risk; but you will struggle to find concrete work based on what he said. In short, he stated that uncertainty is separate from the evaluation of risk. This has an element of appeal to *confidence*, but we have shown that there is uncertainty embedded throughout a risk assessment, and this is probably why his work has not evolved into any practical applications within his core field of economics. However, if we look for more generic models of human decision making, we may find useful approaches.

If we recognise that all human mental processes are laden with uncertainty, then perhaps there is another way of looking at the problem of dealing with uncertainty. This is where we return to the flip-side of the biases discussion from Chapter 3. To understand how there can be a flip-side to biases we need to return to our definition, or assumptions, of rationality.

What is Rationality?

Earlier there was a distinction made between logical and rational. Many may have dismissed this as semantics or other linguistic sleight of hand. The difficulty is that logical is rational, but rational does not have to be logical.

The difference is highlighted when we consider a game invented by economists called *The Ultimatum Game*, a sort of variation on *The Prisoners' Dilemma*. One person is given a sum of money. They are asked to divide the money between themselves and a second person. The first gives the second an ultimatum, "take the offer or leave it." The catch is, if the second person refuses the offer then both sides get nothing. A logical *econ* would accept any offer greater than zero. People tend to refuse any offer lower than a 2/3 to 1/3 split. Useful for social cohesion, and remarkable similar to the 2/3 rule discussed before regarding risk and loss aversion [Haidt].

What if we could remove the emotional input to decision making? This should allow us to function in ways that match the behaviour of *econs*. This does happen, when people suffer damage to the orbitofrontal cortex [Haidt]. However, rather than become ruthless decision machines, these people become paralysed by indecisions, due to the lack of even the slightest preference for choices. Unlike most laboratory experiments that highlight biases they lack the emotional basis to establish the criteria to weigh up options and make a decision. This alone raises questions about the value of the biases model, but even more than that it is the assumption of limits of human thinking that distinguishes differences between rational and logical.

The two are separated by our vision of the capabilities of human thinking. Many of our visions of rationality start with the assumptions that humans have unlimited, or boundless, levels knowledge and an eternity to make a decision. Thus, humans are assumed to have supernatural, or daemonic, powers. A person with these powers would make perfect logical decisions.

Rationality is more complicated than this, as Figure 7 - Visions of Rationality shows. Each of these needs some explanation before we continue on to examine how people deal with decisions in the real world and the *Four Horsemen*.

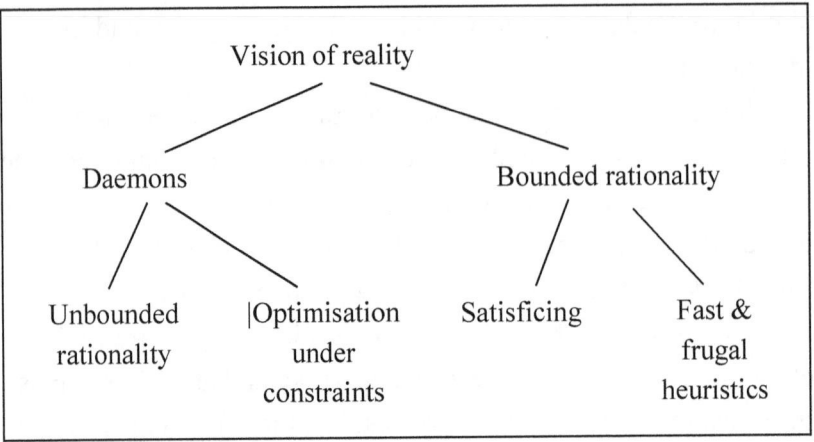

Figure 7 - Visions of Rationality

Daemons

We noted above that one vision of rationality bestows supernatural powers on humans and their ability to make decisions. This takes two flavours; *unbounded rationality* and *optimisation under constraints*. Proponents of the latter would claim that this is an unfair grouping, however, that is addressed below.

Unbounded Rationality

In unbounded rationality there are no restrictions, or constraints placed upon a decision maker. An infinite pool of resources, time, effort and knowledge, are available. The universe is mechanistic and with sufficient effort everything can be analysed with certainty. This school of thought still pervades some discussion, even today, but serious understanding of decision making moved on, with the advent of the mathematics of uncertainty; statistics.

This is the truly divine level of knowledge, because even the concept of Heisenberg's uncertainty principle is removed. With perfect knowledge of every piece of matter and energy, even a coin toss is predictable.

Optimisation under Constraints

The recognition that humans do not have 'divine knowledge' and that there are constraints of time and effort, led to the school of *optimisation under constraints*. Here there is an inclusion of a cost-benefit analysis for the effort required to gain greater certainty. This, however, allows unbounded rationality to slip in via the back-door. How do we know if the effort is worth expending unless we know the value of what we're seeking?

The unbounding often creeps in when we reduce everything to a coin toss or other idealised statistic; like a 1 in 5 chance of losing $100. This is casino gambling and it is the environment that is bound, not the knowledge of the participant. If completed an infinite number of times the results are predictable, hence the knowledge is unbounded.

This ideal, even if unbounded rationality is avoided, forms the basis of most laboratory based research. It spawns the biases that indicate where humans deviate from this ideal. It is comparatively easy to apply to laboratory studies, because the experiment is designed with controlled parameters; except the participants.

If we believe that this is a true reflection of real world experience, then we can stop here. However, the truth is the human decision making is not just constrained, but bound. The difference is more than just semantics.

Bounded Rationality

Bounded rationality is what exists outside the laboratory and structured experiments. It is what we experience every day, but often convince ourselves that in retrospect it was really unbounded, and people were biased in their decisions.

The biases school of thinking assumes that it is human fallibility that causes the deviation from a logical decision. This has been demonstrated in numerous controlled laboratory experiments. The other side of the psychological biases coin is covered by *satisficing* and *fast & frugal heuristics.*

Satisficing and *fast & frugal heuristics* assume a different starting point; uncertainty exists in the 'natural environment' and humans have developed biases and decision making processes to handle this uncertainty. If the bounded rationality assumption is correct, then we may have a way of avoiding the Four Horsemen more often than we should.

In an online forum Khalil Walker described a heuristic as helpful biases and biases as hurtful heuristics. That statement largely underpins the differences between the two schools. If you can hold this dichotomy in mind, as though you are looking at the same thing from a different perspective, then there are fewer sources of conflict.

Satisficing and *fast & frugal heuristics* are reflected in two complementary approaches; *naturalistic decision making* and *ecological rationality*. Both are similar, but have distinct approaches to dealing with decisions under uncertainty. Before examining the work to unite these two camps, we will look at their separate histories and nuanced approaches to how humans handle decisions.

Naturalistic Decision Making

Of the two schools the one that focusses on the idea of *satisficing* is *naturalistic decision making (NDM)*. Satisficing is the concept of finding an answer that is 'satisfactory'; one that meets at least the minimum requirements. Much of the work in this field is binary in the outcomes; live or die; or damage minimisation. The decisions are either/or rather than select the best of a set.

NDM traces its official origin to a conference in 1989. As with all things the truth is the seeds were sown much earlier than this, and was as much a reaction to the failings of the biases school of thought to create a model that explained how people make decisions in "field conditions". This was in specific and deliberate contrast to the laboratory based studies that led to the Kahneman 'biases' school of thinking. This does not mean with no biases rather we need to think of them in a different light.

The early work in this area was funded by the US military in an attempt to ensure more accurate decisions in the bounded field of combat decisions. The researchers adopted a different approach and rather than trying to develop and test a model of decision making, they entered the field and examined how people made decisions. At the 1989 conference Raanan Lipshitz identified nine different models that had developed in parallel.

The most common model in use now dating back to this conference is the *Recognition-Primed Decision Model* (RPM). This model, developed by Gary Klein, started by examining the way firefighting crews approached fires. The model combines experience/intuition and analysis. The experience/intuition is a pattern matching process that is analogous to Kahneman's System 1 (fast and subconscious) while the analysis is analogous to System 2 (deliberate & slow and conscious) [Kahneman].

Unlike the unbounded models, it does not assume that System 1's rapid conclusions are a fault of biases, but a compounding of experience. This is a shift from a domain-independent general approach to a knowledge-based approach. The decision-making process is extended to include a prior stage of perception and recognition of situations, as well as the generation of appropriate responses rather than a selection from given options. This moved decision making to a place that can use cognitive psychology and the cornerstones of this; including scripts, schemas or mental models [Fish (a)].

The basic structure of the RPM is show in Figure 8. The model has a 'recognition' step. Here we might draw a connection between Kahneman's System 1 and the human minds pattern recognition; mentioned earlier in the book. Here our experience has developed models that include cues about dangerous situation and the much faster "red alert" system, which will sense danger in a situation. These models may also include appropriate action to safely exit the situation.

The construction of these mental models can be from both real and synthetic experience. Synthetic experience is a term used to cover all forms of training, including imagining events that have never occurred. The power and benefit of training, and all forms of synthetic experience is unquestionable and the breadth and power is covered in *The Personal Edge* [Fish (a)].

The key feature of this model is that if we have an experience that fits the cues and goals of the situation, we will have an immediate response to how to solve it. This solution may be suboptimal and is often the root of such things as 'not invented here' and other blockers to change; an issue covered in greater depth in *Designing a Better Mousetrap* [Fish (b)].

Sometimes the cues are not a perfect fit to a model, but our System 1 rapidly matches them to a similar pattern. Now we will engage System 2 and run a 'simulation' in our mind of the outcome. If the match is close to a previous experience, that simulation may be very short. However, the less closely the situation under consideration matches our previous experience, the more thinking we will do.

We move through these choices sequentially, rather than as a single massive parallel decision making process. We treat them as simple "will it work" / "won't it work" decisions. We are look for the first choice that satisfies the minimum requirements to achieve a goal, and this is called *satisficing*. The key assumption here is that when resources are limited, we will use this first solution that meets our goals.

Satisficing as a decision process goes some way to explaining suboptimal decisions; especially when combined with the *commitment bias*. However, when resources are limited, but not so limited as to require urgent action and there is the potential to generate several options, this method is unlikely to be the method used. That is the subject of another school of bounded rationality; *fast and frugal heuristics*.

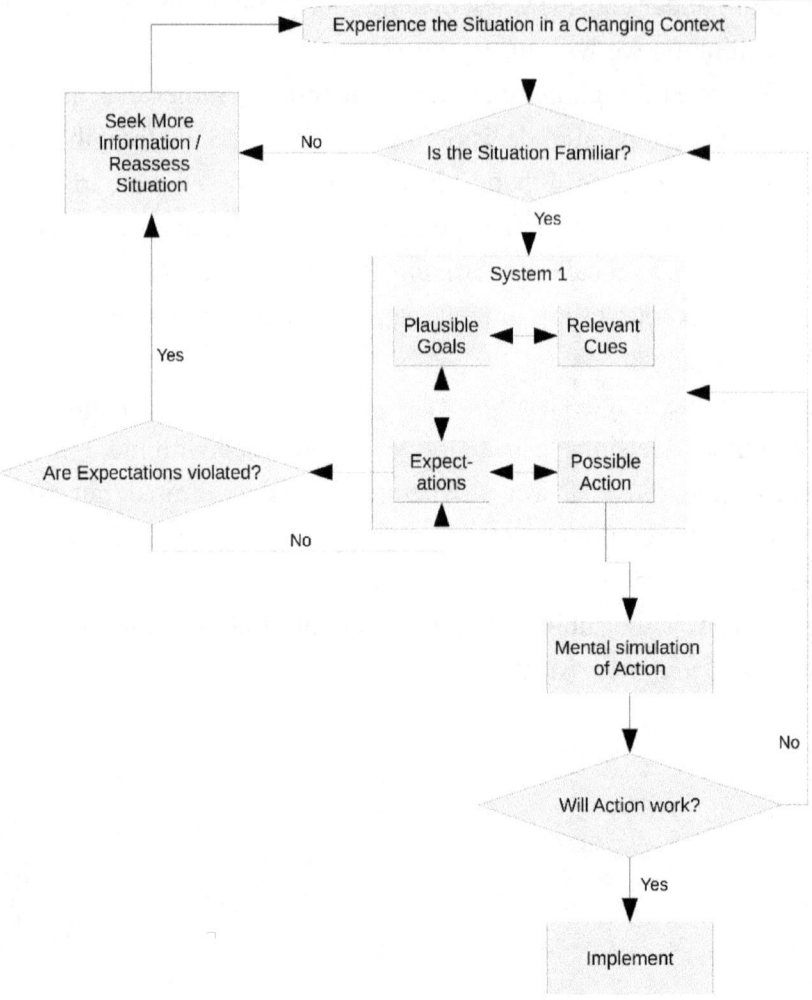

Figure 8 - Recognition Primed Decision Model

(Modified from *Decision Making in Action: Models and Methods* by Klein et al)

Fast and Frugal Heuristics

Fast and Frugal Heuristics are a practical application of the school of *Ecological Rationality*. To better understand this school of thought, it is worth exploring what those two phrases mean. This will not be as easy as it seems which will become clearer as we continue to look at *ecological rationality.*

Fast and Frugal Heuristics (FFH) starts from a slightly different point than NDM, there is a need to decide between at least two things. There are two other underlying presumptions to the FFH model. One is that heuristics are made up of a generic process where each step has alternative methods. The second is that what methods are used out of the "toolbox" depend on the environment; hence the description of being *ecologically rational*. Like NDM it assumes that information is not presented on a platter and the environment will be scanned for cues.

FFH generically have only two steps:

1. Search for cues, and
2. Make a decision.

Zoomed out to this broad level of detail it is almost impossible to distinguish between FFH and NDM. This is not surprising and in truth the two are slowly merging into a single school of thought. The prime difference is that FFH evolved in Europe and NDM in America. Who said politics was dead?

A key philosophical difference between the two camps is the FFH believe in the building block, or modular, principle. This means that a heuristic can be built from a series of other simpler heuristics. Although it is possible to build complex heuristics there are four key classes of heuristic that make up the building blocks.

1. Ignorance based decisions;
2. One reason decisions;
3. Elimination of options; and

4. Satisficing decision.

We can only take a brief look at these, as a full discussion fills the book *Simple Heuristics That Make Us Smart* [Gigerenzer]. The summary below does not do full justice to the ongoing work in this area, which is still being actively researched. The intention is to convey the building blocks and further reading is suggested if you want to know more. However, it should give a flavour of how we decide when the Horsemen are around.

Ignorance based decisions closely matches the NDM model. This is exemplified in the *recognition heuristic*. Do I recognise this situation? Have I done this before and been safe or hurt? When applied to a choice between two options, then the one that is recognised drives the decision. This can be extended to a more complex multiple option scenario, which shows the 'modular' nature of FFH.

What if there are several options are available? If only one is recognised that suits the goal, then it is the obvious choice, but what if more than one option is recognised? This is the point at which we would look for relevant cues that experience tells us distinguish between the options. The selection of the cues maybe done using a recognition heuristic; demonstrating how these decision process can nest within each other.

The *one reason decision* is a close variant of the recognition heuristic. However, rather than just picking something we recognise we look for a cue that exceeds a threshold value. But what cue do we use? Three simple heuristics have been developed:
1. Take the Best,
2. Take the Last, and
3. Minimalist.

Take the Best uses our previous experience, and we use cues that have led to successful decisions in the past. Take the Last uses the cue we used last time we made a successful   ?   in this field. Minimalist uses cues in a random order. Looking at these approaches, it is easy to envisage how as we learn we use them in the reverse of the order they are listed. It may also explain why our experience might lead us to a different 'best cue' for a decision. One person may have success using one cue whilst another had selected another, whilst moving up the list had initially selected another cue and had success with that one. Then what happens when the two people discuss a decision but have different cues that suggest different courses of action? Already we can model complex thinking with a few simple rules; as network designers have discovered by examining ant behaviour.

These heuristics have been tested in simulations against more intense mathematical methods; including linear regression. Surprisingly, these heuristics can come close to and even exceed the accuracy of their more 'logical' brethren. This is a plausible explanation as to why experts can outperform complex computer simulations.

These heuristics are thought to also play a role in memory reconstruction. When we review our memories, we use our experience, sometimes of post events cues, to rationalise our decisions and confabulate a self-supporting story [Fish (b)]. This leads to 20/20 hindsight, or *hindsight bias*. It could also be the way we progress up the heuristic models by reviewing our experiences, to decide which cues have or might have given the best prediction of the outcome.

Most *elimination heuristics* are a form of *one reason* methods, but applied repeatedly. In essence, we work through cues to see if we should keep an option as a possibility or eliminate it. We repeat this until we are left with a single option.

We met the idea of *satisficing* above with NDM. Under FFH satisficing has a more specific application. Here it is used when time is not significantly limited. As before this is about finding an option that satisfies some minimum criteria. The reasoning with respect time is vague, and it is more a condition of options presenting themselves sequentially. Placing less emphasis on time and concentrating on sequential presentation then the NDM model is the equivalent of this.

All of these heuristics work, and often outperform more complex methods, because they take advantage of the ecology of the natural environment. The choice of heuristic depends on the characteristic of the environment.

The *one reason* approach works well where using more than one cue makes little difference to the 'correctness' of the choice. The *one reason* approach, also, excels when information is scarce and there are few cues relative to the number of options. These are situations where the Four Horsemen are likely to be rampant.

The *elimination* approach works when there are Power Law distributions, sometimes referred to as J-curves, define the likelihood of an outcome. It has been argued by Nassim Taleb in *The Black Swan* that these are more common than we often consider them to be [Taleb]. This may explain why the self-trained expert can outperform sophisticated computer models.

The *satisficing* approach works when there are an ever-decreasing number of options available. Whether this be due to changes in the environment or, as in NDM, by mental modelling. Thus, the options could be change passively, or due to other people's decisions, or by active elimination by the decider.

The power of these heuristics is their robustness. Once effective cues have been developed for a situation type then we can make effective decisions, even when we are uncertain about a large amount of the data. Perhaps they are how we have evaded the Horsemen for so long.

Chapter 6
The Four Horsemen in Action

The clearest way to show the *Four Horsemen*, and their close friends the *Three Kings*, in action is to look at an example of a risk assessment. The risk assessment here is based on a real life example that illustrates the points made in this book. Although it is simplified in some ways to disguise its origins, all the steps are as they were when it was submitted for review by the company's senior management. The steps are the same for any risk assessment (quantified decision) and you can look for the analogies to the decision process you normally use.

Crossing the River

The example is about the risk of a pipeline that crosses a river near the entrance to a port being damaged by a ship's anchor. To reach the port ships must pass over the pipeline. Under normal circumstances this is no problem. However, if a vessel needs to wait for a berth to be free or has an unexpected failure then they will drop anchor and this can damage the pipeline.

As we build up the risk assessment we will see how, and where, the *Four Horsemen* trot into the workings. With this example you should be able to more critically examine risk assessments before you trust the numbers and remember to use a tried and tested heuristic to make the decision.

The first place to look for a start to the assessment is if there is data for anchor damage to pipelines. The UK maintains a database of anchor damage called the PARLOC database. We could feel that we have sidestepped the whole issue of uncertainty with this hard data, but in truth the first King has brought us the gift of *representativeness*. He has, also, hidden the aleatory error in the model used to compile the database; all the hidden assumptions used when collating the information. However, we need to look more closely at the data available.

A careful reading of the report shows that there is a lack of data thus we cannot avoid uncertainty in the values quoted. The report recognises this and quotes upper and lower values of likelihood; as any good statistical analysis should. However, this is just *Famine* sideling in while we look the other way and use the average value.

Now we need to take a closer look at the data. There is not any data that covers the specific scenario we are investigating. Many involve supply or maintenance ships anchoring near offshore platforms. There are some that are close in definition to our scenario and at best we can take the data as ambiguous; hence *War* has come to the risk assessment, laying waste to our confidence in its accuracy.

We can counter-attack *War's* presence by making some assumptions about how these relate to our situation. This, however, is only a substitution of *Famine* for *War*. We are substituting our 'reasonable' assumptions for the ill-fitting facts we have at hand; no matter how much our assumptions are guided by the data at hand. In fact, we are more likely to experience the presence of one of the *Three Kings, Anchoring*, rather than be completely subjective. This may make our subjective assessment better than a complete guess, but it has only diminished *Famine* not banished it.

We could try decomposing the problem into smaller groups of events; as it is generally easier to make estimates of more specific events than for more general ones. Again, this is a subtle exchange of one horseman for another; in this case *Pestilence* for *War*. In fact, the biggest danger is that both *Pestilence* and *War* enter and further confuse the validity of the numbers.

Next we need to know what the *outcome* of the event is; having only examined the likelihood. Where do we start? Small vessels will not damage the pipeline, so we need only consider larger ones. But how many people might die? How many are on a ship? Is it 5, 10 or 20? Whatever value we select it will be a mean, median or typical AND wrong. *Famine* has quietly become our friend.

Clearly a range of values are all potentially valid and we could try further to justify our choices with Monte Carlo analysis or other simulations. None will hide the truth that we are uncertain about the "true value".

Our next step is to see what risk reduction the measure we could implement might achieve. *Famine* and *War* reside here hidden in plain sight. The measures under consideration are to reduce human error, and are notoriously difficult to justify. Without resorting to the numbers trust me when I say that the risk was deemed *tolerable* and did not justify any new, expensive and ineffective measure to reduce the likelihood of the event. But could we have taken a less comprehensive approach with less subtle uncertainty and trusted a heuristic to direct our decision?

Let us assume that the pipeline has been constructed to standards that time has shown to be *tolerable*. We can embrace the uncertainty and use 'conservative' value for the likelihood of a fatal event. This would give us the largest potential for risk reduction and equates to a larger potential expenditure available to

81

reduce risk. For a fuller explanation of why this is so read the UK HSE's web page on Cost-Benefit Analysis.

Even with this larger pot of money the expenditure was not "clearly" justified by the cost-benefit analysis. So, did the longer, and notionally more accurate risk assessment vindicate the effort?

People that make decisions based on efforts to reduce human error know that the numbers do not always reflect our "gut feeling". That "gut feeling" is our *system 1, fast thinking heuristic* making a judgement. A wholly inexplicable sense that the risk reduction is optimistic tells us that the expenditure is not value for money.

The only problem left with using the simple and quick heuristic to come to this conclusion? We have entered the error of scientific decision making; or more importantly litigation avoidance; that requires us to support our decision with numbers. Even if we know those numbers are vague and uncertain.

Chapter 7
Closing Thoughts

We started by examining all the ways that uncertainty creeps into our risk assessments and finished by looking at models that explain how we make decisions despite this uncertainty. At the start it seemed as if accurate risk assessments are impossible, found possible reasons why we get them wrong and then how our decision making processes counter the uncertainty.

Uncertainty permeates everything we do, because in reality every decision we make is a risk based decision. We cannot escape it. We may wish to delude ourselves and pretend that things are not uncertain, but that is only true in simple "games of chance".

Uncertainty comes when our question is unclear, or the assumptions we make are not perfectly defined, then the *King of Availability* is different on both sides of a discussion. *War* lurks in this ambiguity and conflict over the meaning of our numbers is inevitable.

Sometimes our question, or analysis, becomes complex and we invite *Pestilence* in to rot at our understanding. When we are unclear what impact small changes in our assumptions, or our model, have then we encourage only confusion. Doubt, if not cast in our own mind, will certainly be cast on anyone using the analysis.

In real life, we do not know everything as well as we might think. We make subjective assumptions about data and this is the hallmark of *Famine*. This lack of solid data, typically replaced by experience, creates a clear space to question the validity of any decision.

There is uncertainty in everything we use and *Death* awaits every potential decision. There are many subtle forms of uncertainty in almost everything we use to make risk assessments, and these hinder consensus in some decisions and support accusations of bias in others.

There is a plethora of biases that creep in to human decision making when compared to a purely logical decision. These biases only show up in simple laboratory experiments, and are extrapolated into more general situations that still contain low levels of uncertainty. The question is not whether we have these biases, rather it is knowing that they confer an advantage when there is uncertainty at a greater level.

One school of thought takes the perspective that these biases are rules we use to make decisions where uncertainty is present. They allow us to make effective decisions under uncertainty that are close or as effective, as more sophisticated models that are built from the statistical/logical assumption.

Where does this leave us? Any risk assessment we make, numerical or qualitative, we know is inaccurate, which is a polite way of saying wrong. However, we are learning that our decision-making processes, or heuristics, may be such that we can still make 'good decisions' despite the embedded uncertainty.

The quality of decisions achieved by the fast & frugal heuristics, also, suggests that we often need to stop trying to improve the quality of the values in the risk assessment and look at the issue of gains or losses from both party's perspective. It is more a question of our bias in the interpretation of the outcome that may be more influential than any other aspect of the decision.

We should learn to embrace the uncertainty in our world and come to accept we can still make decisions. The risk assessment may be wrong, but that does not mean the decision is. A less uncertain risk assessment might also mean that you get no better a decision and that experience may be more of a help than we give it credit for, but might, also, create too much confidence in our own subjectivity.

Go back to your day job, fight analysis paralysis and trust your decision making instincts, but listen to other people, too.

Further Reading

John Hollman; (presentation) Risk Analysis at the Edge of Chaos (AACEI)

Taleb, Nassim Nicholas. *The Black Swan: The Impact of the Highly Improbable*. New York: Random House, 2007. Print.

Stavros N; *Interpreting uncertainty when making decisions*; TedxTalk; tedxtalks.ted.com

Knight, F.H. (1921): Risk, uncertainty and profit. Houghton Mifflin, Boston

Haidt, Jonathan. *The Happiness Hypothesis: Finding Modern Truth in Ancient Wisdom*. New York: Basic, 2006. Print.

Kahneman, Daniel. *Thinking, Fast and Slow*. New York: Farrar, Straus and Giroux, 2015. Print.

Hirschman, Elizabeth C., Daniel Kahneman, Paul Slovic, and Amos Tversky. "Judgement under Uncertainty: Heuristics and Biases." *Journal of Marketing Research* 20.2 (1983): 217. Web.

Gigerenzer, Gerd, and Peter M. Todd. Simple Heuristics That Make Us Smart. New York: Oxford UP, 2001. Print.

(CCPS), Center for Chemical Process Safety. *Guidelines for Risk Based Process Safety*. New York: Wiley, 2011. Print.

CCPS. *Guidelines for Chemical Process Quantitative Risk Analysis*. New York: AICHE. Print.

Wilhelmsen, Cheryl A., and Lee T. Ostrom. *Risk Assessment Tools, Techniques, and Their Applications*. Hoboken, NJ: Wiley, 2012. Print.

CCPS. *Guidelines for Developing Quantitative Safety Risk Criteria*. John Wiley & Sons, 2009. Print.

Humphreys, Kenneth K. *Project and Cost Engineers' Handbook*. New York: Marcel Dekker, 2005. Print.

Bibliography

John Hollman; (presentation) Risk Analysis at the Edge of Chaos (AACEI)

Fish (a), E.J.; The Personal Edge

Fish (b), E.J.; Designing a Better Mousetrap

Fish (c), E.J.; The Management Assumption

Taleb, Nassim Nicholas. *The Black Swan: The Impact of the Highly Improbable*. New York: Random House, 2007. Print.

Stavros N; *Interpreting Uncertainty When Making Decisions*; TedxTalk; tedxtalks.ted.com

Knight, F.H. (1921): Risk, Uncertainty and Profit. Houghton Mifflin, Boston

Haidt, Jonathan. *The Happiness Hypothesis: Finding Modern Truth in Ancient Wisdom*. New York: Basic, 2006. Print.

Kahneman, Daniel. *Thinking, Fast and Slow*. New York: Farrar, Straus and Giroux, 2015. Print.

Hirschman, Elizabeth C., Daniel Kahneman, Paul Slovic, and Amos Tversky. "Judgement under Uncertainty: Heuristics and Biases." *Journal of Marketing Research* 20.2 (1983): 217. Web.

Gigerenzer, Gerd, and Peter M. Todd. Simple Heuristics That Make Us Smart. New York: Oxford UP, 2001. Print.

List of Contributors

The single biggest contributor to this book was Anne Adams, who for reasons best known only to herself took on the editorial duties and suffered to learn a lot about risk along the way. The need to stop and clarify my explanations to her prevented me assuming too much about the reader's level of understanding.

A lifelong friend Ian Brown kept me aware of the need to have a life, when I got obsessive. This no doubt improved the quality of the work.

Index